ECCE VENIT
Behold He Cometh

A. J. GORDON

Published by Left of Brain Books

Copyright © 2021 Left of Brain Books

ISBN 978-1-396-31796-5

First Edition

All rights reserved. No part of this publication may be reproduced, distributed, or transmitted in any form or by any means, including photocopying, recording, or other electronic or mechanical methods, without the prior written permission of the publisher, except in the case of brief quotations embodied in critical reviews and certain other noncommercial uses permitted by copyright law. Left of Brain Books is a division of Left of Brain Onboarding Pty Ltd.

Table of Contents

Preface.	1
PART I. FORETOLD.	3
I. The Uplifted Gaze.	5
II. Tarrying Within the Veil.	11
III. The Power of His Coming.	20
IV. The Programme of Redemption.	28
V. The Ends of the Ages.	36
PART II. FORFEITED.	47
I. Heavenly Citizenship.	49
II. The Fall of the Church.	55
III. The Advent of Antichrist.	62
IV. The Bride of Antichrist.	75
V. The Mock Millennium.	83
VI. The Eclipse of Hope.	93
PART III. FULFILLED.	100
I. Hope Revived.	102
II. Foregleams of the Day.	110
III. Behold He Cometh!	118
IV. The First Resurrection.	123
V. The Translation of the Church.	133
VI. The Marriage of the Lamb.	140
VII. The Judgment of Christendom.	145
VIII. The Restoration of Israel.	154
IX. The Millennial Kingdom.	162

PREFACE.

THE importance of a doctrine may be judged somewhat by the proportionate space and prominence given to it in the New Testament. Measured by this standard, the theme of Christ's coming in glory is second to none in Scripture, not even to the atonement itself, in the claim which it makes upon our consideration. "*A real pearl of Christian truth and knowledge,*" a great expositor calls it. And since the merchantmen who seek this goodly pearl are too few, it becomes those who have proved it, both by spiritual experience and scriptural study, to be indeed a "pearl of great price," to do their utmost to set forth its excellency. If, therefore, in what we have written we have reflected one "purest ray serene" from this precious doctrine and glorious hope of the Church, we shall count it a high honor from the Lord.

Would that such a theme might be divested of all controversial aspects! But here, as everywhere, there are schools of interpretation between which one finds himself obliged, whether he will or not, to choose. Pre-millennial or post-millennial advent—Christ's coming before the millennium or after the millennium—is the issue which divides two great parties of biblical students. We humbly but firmly hold with the first school on this question. If we admit, with the eminent theologian Van Oosterzee,—to whom we acknowledge great indebtedness,—that "some courage is required to range one's self among the defenders of Chiliasm," with him we profess that "we do so nevertheless in obedience to faith in the Word, without which we know nothing of the future." And yet here the courage of conviction need not be greatly taxed considering these two facts, viz., that the concession of Church historians, led by such masters as Neander and Harnack, is that pre-millennialism was the orthodox and accepted faith of the Church in the primitive and purest ages; and that the opinion of the most eminent exegetes of our time, that this is the true doctrine of Scripture, so strongly preponderates as to give promise of an early practical *consensus.*

Pre-millenarians, again, are divided into two schools, the Futurist and the Historical: the former of whom hold that Antichrist is yet to appear, and that the larger part of the Apocalypse remains to be fulfilled; while the latter maintains, with the reformers and the expositors of the early post-Reformation era, that Antichrist has already come in the bloody and blasphemous system of the papacy, and that the Apocalypse has been continuously fulfilling from our Lord's ascension to the present time. If we turn away from the Futurist interpretation—in which we were "nourished and brought up" so far as our prophetic studies are concerned—and express our firm adherence to the Historical, it is because we believe that the latter is more scriptural, and rests upon the more obvious and simple interpretation of the Word; and also because we find that it has such verifications in fulfilled history and chronology as to compel even some of its strongest opponents to concede that it is a true interpretation if not the complete and final one. But we deprecate controversy between these schools, since both hold strongly to the hope of the Lord's imminent return, and are vying with each other in earnest endeavor to restore the doctrine to its true place in the creed and in the consciousness of the Church. It certainly becomes us all, while rejoicing in the light we have, humbly to wait for greater light, assured that, in the foregleams of the approaching advent, contradictions will more and more vanish, till in our gathering together unto Him "the watchmen shall lift up the voice, with the voice together shall they sing, for they shall see eye to eye when the Lord shall bring again Zion."

When Samuel Taylor Coleridge had finished reading that remarkable book, Ben Ezra's "Coming of Messiah in Glory and Majesty," he indited the following prayer. With its devout aspirations in our hearts and on our lips, let us come to the study of the exalted theme.

> *"O Almighty God, Absolute Good, Eternal I Am! Ground of my being, Author of my existence, and its ultimate end! mercifully cleanse my heart, enlighten my understanding, and strengthen my will; that if it be needful or furtherant to the preparation of my soul, and of Thy Church, for the advent of Thy kingdom, that I should be led into the right belief respecting the second coming of the Son of man into the world, the eye of my mind may be quickened into quietness and singleness of sight. Amen."*

CLARENDON STREET CHURCH, BOSTON,
September 1, 1889

PART I.

FORETOLD.

"This word He has in fact spoken,—'Hereafter ye shall see the Son of man coming in the clouds of heaven,'—but it is a word of which there is no other example. Even the mad pride of Roman emperors who demanded religious homage for their statues has never gone so far to conceive such an unheard-of thought, and here it is the lowliest among men who speaks. The word must be truth; for there is here no mean term between the truth and madness."

LUTHARDT.

Ὅτι αὐτὸς Ὁ Κύριος ἐν κελεύσματι, ἐν φωνῇ ἀρχαγγέλου, καὶ ἐν σάλπιγγι θεοῦ καταβήσεται ἀπ' οὐρανοῦ.

PAUL, 1 Thess. iv

I.
THE UPLIFTED GAZE.

HAVE we thought how significant and full of instruction is the earliest attitude of the Church as presented in the opening chapter of the Acts: "Ye men of Galilee, *why stand ye gazing up into heaven?*" In a single graphic sentence is thus indicated the primitive uplook of Christianity; and this question, with what immediately follows, is uttered, not so much for rebuke as for interpretation. The great High Priest has just passed within the veil, and the cloud-curtain has shut Him out of sight. And, as the Hebrew congregation, upon the great day of atonement, looked steadfastly upon the receding form of Aaron as he disappeared within the veil, and continued looking long after he was out of sight, waiting for his reappearance; so exactly did these men of Galilee, though they knew not what they did. And the angels were sent to declare to them the meaning of their action: "*This same Jesus, which is taken up from you into heaven, shall so come in like manner as ye have seen Him go into heaven.*" This is the earliest post-ascension announcement of that gospel of hope which, at the first, began to be spoken by the Lord Himself,—"*If I go . . . I will come again*"—which is now confirmed unto us by His angels, and is henceforth to be reiterated by apostle and seer till, from the last page of Revelation, it shall be heard sounding forth its "*Surely I come quickly.*"

The second coming of Christ is the crowning event of redemption; and the belief of it constitutes the crowning article of an evangelical creed. For we hold that the excellence of faith is according to the proportion of the Lord's redemptive work which that faith embraces. Some accept merely the earthly life of Christ, knowing Him only after the flesh; and the religion of such is rarely more than a cold, external morality. Others receive His vicarious death and resurrection, but seem not to have strength as yet to follow Him into the heavens; such may be able to rejoice in their justification without knowing much of walking in the glorified life of Christ. Blessed are they who, believing all that has gone before,—life, death, and resurrection,—can joyfully add this confession also: "*We have a great High Priest who is passed through the heavens*;" and thrice blessed they who can join to this confession still another: "*From whence also we look for the Saviour, the Lord Jesus Christ.*" For it is the essential part of our Redeemer's priesthood that, having entered in, to make intercession for His people, He shall again come forth to bless them. How sweet was the sound of the golden bells upon the high priest's garments, issuing from the holy of holies, and telling the waiting congregation of Israel that, though invisible, he was still alive, bearing their names upon his breastplate, and offering up prayers for them, before God! But, though they listened intently to these reassuring sounds from within the veil, they watched with steadfast gaze for his reappearing, and for the benediction of his uplifted hands that should tell of their acceptance.[1] This they counted the crowning act of his ministration. Therefore, says the Son of Sirach, "How glorious was he before the multitude of his people, in his coming forth from within the veil! He was as the morning star in the midst of the cloud, or as the moon when her days are full." If this could be said of the typical high priest, how much more of the true! Glorious beyond description will be His reëmergence from the veil; "the bright and morning Star," breaking forth from behind the cloud that received Him out of sight; His once pierced hands lifted in benediction above His Church, while that shall be fulfilled which is written in the Hebrews: "And when He again bringeth in the Firstborn into the world, He saith, And let all the angels of God worship Him" (Heb. i. 6, R. V.).

This attitude of the men of Galilee became the permanent attitude of the primitive Church; so that the apostle's description of the Thessalonian Christians—"Ye turned to God from idols, to serve the living and true God, and *to wait for His Son from Heaven*"—might apply equally to all. Talk we of "the notes of a true Church"? Here is one of the most unquestionable,— the uplifted gaze. As apostate Christianity, by a perverse instinct, is perpetually aping the eastward posture of Paganism (Ezekiel viii. 16), so inevitably is apostolic Christianity constantly recurring to the upward posture of Primitivism. What Tholuck says of Israel, that, "As no other nation of antiquity, it is a people of expectation," is equally true of the Church of the New Testament. It is anchored upward, not downward; its drawing is forward, not backward; "Which hope we have as an anchor of the

---

[1] "All their hopes depended on his life within the veil; and when at length he came forth alone, there was great joy, for they thought they were accepted."—*Gemara*.

soul, both sure and steadfast, and which entereth into that within the veil, whither the forerunner is for us entered, even Jesus." As the ancient *Anchorius* bore the anchor into port, and fastened it there, while as yet the ship could not enter, because of the tide; so has our *Prodromos*—our Precursor—fixed the Church's hold within the veil, that it may not drift away through adverse winds or tides. But this anchoring is only a preparation for that entering which He shall effect for us when He shall come again to receive us unto Himself.

What if those who are much occupied with looking up, zealous to "come behind in no gift, *waiting for the coming of the Lord,*" should sometimes be stigmatized as star-gazers and impracticable dreamers? Let them rejoice that, in so acting, they prove themselves, not only the sons of primitive Christianity, but also the sons of primitive humanity. For, in the beginning, God made man upright, both physically and morally. Some tell us that the derivation of ἄνθρωπος—man—makes the word signify an uplooker.[2] Certainly, this originally constituted his marked distinction from the brutes that perish, that, while they looked downwards towards the earth, which is their goal, he looked upward toward the heaven for which he was predestined. How significant the question which Jehovah puts to the first sinner of Adam's sons: " *Why is thy countenance fallen?*" The wages of sin is death, and the goal of the sinner is the earth with its narrow house. So we find the whole apostate race, from the earliest transgressor onward, with countenance downcast and shadowed with mortality, moving toward the tomb and unable to lift up the eyes. But the sons of the second Adam appear looking steadfastly up to heaven and saying: "We see Jesus, who was made a little lower than the angels, for the suffering of death, crowned with glory and honor." His coronation has restored their aspiration: it has lifted their gaze upward once more to the throne.

The tabernacle imagery is still further suggestive touching the subject under consideration. Ask the ritualist, clothed in his rich vestments, and offering his eucharistic sacrifice upon the altar, why he does thus; and the answer is, that the minister must repeat in the Church on earth what our Great High Priest is doing in the true tabernacle above. But if this principle were faithfully carried out, it would prove the death-warrant of ritualism. The great

---

[2] "From this circumstance—man's elevated countenance—the Greeks plainly derived the name ἄνθρωπος, because he looks upward."—Lactantius, *Inst.* ii. 1.

day of atonement is now passing; let all sacrifices and services cease without the veil. Oh, ye self-ordained priests, why do ye "*stand* daily ministering and offering, oftentimes, the same sacrifices which can never take away sins?" Behold, "this Man, after he had offered one sacrifice for sins forever, *sat down* on the right hand of God, *from henceforth expecting* till His foes be made His footstool." They most literally reflect His ministry on earth who, at the communion, *sit down* to remember the sacrifice of Calvary, but not to repeat it; who listen to the "Till He come," which it whispers, and so unite with Him in His "expecting." He waits for the same event for which He bids us wait, His triumphal return. And for the congregation before the veil, not worship, but work and witnessing, are now the principal calling,—work and witnessing with special reference to that glorious consummation which our Saviour is anticipating. For, as He assigns us our service, this is the language of His commission: "*Occupy till I come*;" and, as He appoints us our testimony, this is the purport of it: "And this gospel of the Kingdom shall be preached in all the world, for a witness to all nations; *and then shall the end come.*"

Indeed, let us observe that, since Christ took His place of expectancy within the veil, and assigned us our place of expectancy without the veil, all present duties and spiritual exercises have henceforth an onward look; an advent adjustment, like the needle to the pole. "The solemn Maranatha resounds throughout the Scriptures, and forms the key-note in all their exhortations, consolations, warnings."[3] Is holy living urged? This is the inspiring motive thereto: "That, denying ungodliness and worldly lusts, we should live soberly, righteously, and godly in this present world, *looking for that blessed hope and the glorious appearing of the great God and our Saviour Jesus Christ*" (Titus ii. 13). Is endurance under persecution and loss of goods enjoined? This is the language of the exhortation: "Cast not away, therefore, your confidence, which hath great recompense of reward. *For yet a little while and He that shall come will come and will not tarry*" (Heb. x. 35-37). Is patience under trial encouraged in the Christian? The admonition is: "Be ye also patient; stablish your hearts, *for the coming of the Lord draweth nigh*" (James v. 8). Is sanctification set before us for our diligent seeking? The duties leading up to it culminate in this: "And the very God of peace sanctify you

---

[3] Van Oosterzee.

wholly; and I pray God your whole spirit and soul and body be preserved blameless *at the coming of our Lord Jesus Christ*" (1 Thess. v. 23). Is diligence in caring for the flock of God enjoined upon pastors? This is the reward: "Feed the flock of God which is among you, taking the oversight thereof, not by constraint, but willingly; . . . *and when the Chief Shepherd shall appear, ye shall receive a crown of glory that fadeth not away*" (1 Peter v. 4). Is fidelity to the gospel trust charged upon the ministry? This is the end thereof: "That thou keep this commandment without spot, unrebukable, *until the appearing of our Lord Jesus Christ*" (1 Tim. vi. 14). And again: "I charge thee in the sight of God and of Christ Jesus, who shall judge the quick and the dead, *and by His appearing and His kingdom,* preach the word" (2 Tim. iv. 1). Space would fail us, indeed, to cite passages of this purport; they so abound that we may say that the key to which the chief exhortations to service and consecration are pitched in the New Testament is: "To the end He may stablish your hearts unblamable in holiness before God, even our Father, *at the coming of our Lord Jesus Christ with all His saints*" (1 Thess. iii. 13).

The reader of these and many other texts of like import will observe how God has thus marked His admonitions with the rising inflection, as though to save our Christian living from depression and monotony. Duty done for duty's sake becomes commonplace; activity inspired by the possible nearness of death has a certain downward emphasis unbecoming the children of the kingdom. Therefore duty—that which is due—is less insisted on in the gospel, as a motive, than reward,—that which may be attained; and as for the imminence of death as an inspiration to devotedness, we never find it once mentioned. It is the advent of the King of glory, "*Behold, I come quickly*; and My reward is with Me to give to every man according as his work shall be," and not the advent of the kings of terrors, that constitutes the incentive to Christian earnestness. However low the note which is struck in God's discipline of His people, it is always keyed to a lofty pitch to which it is certain to rise; and if, as in one familiar instance, the inspired discourse drops to the ground-tones of death and doom,—"*It is appointed unto men once to die, but after this the judgment*"—it is only that it may mount immediately to the exalted strain to which the whole New Testament is tuned,—"So Christ was once offered to bear the sins of many, and unto them that look for Him *shall He appear a second time without sin unto salvation*" (Heb. ix. 28).

Never did a Christian age so greatly need to have its attitude readjusted to the primitive standard as our own,—commerce, so debased with greed of gold; science, preaching its doctrine of "dust thou art;" and Christian dogmatics, often darkening hope with its eschatology of death! The face of present-day religion is to such degree prone downward that, if some Joseph appears, with his visions of the sun, moon, and stars, men exclaim: "Behold, this dreamer cometh." But they that say such things plainly declare that they *do not* "seek a country." There is a tradition that Michael Angelo, by his prolonged and unremitting toil upon the frescoed domes which he wrought, acquired such a habitual upturn of the countenance that, as he walked the streets, strangers would observe his bearing, and set him down as some visionary or eccentric. It were well if we who profess to be Christians of the apostolic school had our conversation so truly in heaven, and our faces so steadfastly set thitherward, that sometimes the "man with the muck-rake" should be led to wonder at us, and to look up with questioning surprise from his delving for earthly gold and glory. Massillon declares that, "in the days of primitive Christianity, it would have been deemed a kind of apostasy not to sigh for the return of the Lord." Then, certainly, it ought not now to be counted an eccentricity to "love His appearing," and to take up with new intensity of longing the prayer which He has taught us: "Even so, come Lord Jesus." Amid all the disheartenment induced by the abounding iniquity of our times; amid the loss of faith and the waxing cold of love within the Church; and amid the outbreaking of lawlessness without, causing men's hearts to fail them for fear, and for looking after those things that are coming on the earth,—this is our Lord's inspiring exhortation: "Look up and lift up your heads, for your redemption draweth nigh."

II.
TARRYING WITHIN THE VEIL.

CENTURIES have passed since our great High Priest disappeared behind the cloud-curtain of the heavenly sanctuary; and His Church, like the people of old who waited for Zacharias, has "marvelled that He tarrieth so long in the temple." Pondering the sacred promises of His return, which are written for our hope, we find warnings of startling immediateness, but also mysterious suggestions of possible long delay. In the post-ascension gospel of Revelation, the word is constantly sounding out, "*Behold, I come quickly*;" while in the parables of the kingdom, contained in the closing chapters of the Gospel according to Matthew, we read, "*While the Bridegroom tarried*," and "*After a long time*, the Lord of those servants cometh and reckoneth with them." Yet both of these gospels have the same key-note: "*Watch, therefore*, for ye know neither the day nor the hour wherein the Son of man cometh" (Matt. xxv. 13); and "*Blessed is he that watcheth* and keepeth his garments" (Rev. xvi. 15). Hence we conclude that these texts are parts of a complex system of prophecy, wherein incitements to hope and checks to impatience are so perfectly balanced as to keep the Church ever expectant, while restraining her from being ever despondent. For nothing can be plainer to the unprejudiced reader of the New Testament than that it is the purpose of the ascended Bridegroom to have his Bride constantly, soberly, and busily waiting for His return, until the appointed time of His detention in the heavens shall have expired.[4] Hence "He has harmonized with consummate skill every part of His revelation to produce this general result; now speaking as if a few seasons more were to herald the new earth, now as if His days were thousands of years; at one moment whispering into the ear of His disciple, at another retreating into the depth of infinite ages. It is His purpose thus to live in our faith and hope, remote yet near, pledged to no moment, possible at any; worshipped, not with

---

[4] "The heaven that gives back Christ gives back all we have loved and lost, solves all doubts, and ends all sorrows. His coming looks in upon the whole life of His Church, as a lofty mountain peak looks in upon every little valley and sequestered home about its base, and belongs to them all alike. Every generation lies under the shadow of it."—Rev. John Ker.

the consternation of a near, or the indifference of a distant, certainty, but with the anxious vigilance that awaits a contingency ever at hand. This, the deep devotion of watchfulness, humility, and awe, He who knows us best knows to be the fittest posture of our spirits; therefore does He preserve the salutary suspense that ensures it, and therefore will He determine His advent to no definite day in the calendar of eternity."[5]

How could revelation be so adjusted as to secure this end—the perpetual watchfulness of the Church for the Redeemer's second coming—without, in the event of long delay, subjecting the Lord to the imputation of having deceived His flock, or the inspired apostles to the charge of being mistaken in the hopes which they cherished for themselves, and which they nourished in those to whom they wrote? We shall find the true answer to these questions by searching the Scripture to learn how God has actually effected this result.

Observe, in the first place, the union of the known and the unknown in this great problem of the advent consummation; a union exactly fitted to inspire the Church with sacred curiosity to search diligently and constantly for its solution. For just as there is in revelation a dogmatic certainty as to the fact of Christ's return, "*The Lord Himself shall descend from heaven with a shout,*" so there is a dogmatic uncertainty as to the time of His return: "*But of that day and that hour knoweth no man, no, not the angels which are in heaven, neither the Son, but the Father.*" By this combination of the revealed and the unrevealed, perennial interest and inspiring search are ensured, which were utterly impossible if either one of these elements were wanting. Take away the certainty as to the fact of Christ's coming, and tell us that He may never return, and at once the wing of hope is paralyzed, and the eye of vigilance closed; take away the uncertainty as to the time of Christ's coming, and tell us that a definite thousand years of millennial blessedness stands between us and the advent; or have told the early disciples that at least eighteen centuries must elapse before their Lord should come back,—and looking for His immediate return were utterly impossible, so that the watchman's vigil must cease and the virgin's lamp be quenched. Therefore, by a wise combining of the known and the unknown factors in the construction of prophecy, there have been

---

[5] Archer Butler.

secured the most powerful stimulant to watchfulness, and the most salutary check to presumption.

By the succession of prophetic fulfilments the same result is promoted. It is a part of the divine plan to give an onward look to all predestined events; prophecy no sooner becomes history than history in turn becomes prophecy, accomplished facts passing into foretypes of greater facts to come. "A little while and ye shall not see Me," said Jesus in His last discourse with His disciples, "*and again a little while and ye shall see Me*" (John xvi. 16). After two days of burial they did see Him, coming forth from the grave, and ending the "little while" of their lonely separation in the joy of the resurrection fellowship. But the forty days of risen earthly life soon terminated and He went to the Father, and again they saw Him not. Yet after another "little while" of waiting the day of Pentecost arrived; and then, as the Holy Ghost descended, they beheld Him again *spiritually*, as He had promised,—ὄψεσθε με. Thus was His word fulfilled: "I will not leave you orphans; *I will come to you*." But the end of the Master's gracious prediction had not been reached: the expectation had rather been lifted up and carried on, through what Stier calls "*the typico-prophetical perspective*" of this prediction, to that still further coming in which these others were to find their consummation. Therefore the writer of the Epistle to the Hebrews, addressing those who had "tasted the heavenly gift" and been made "partakers of the Holy Ghost," takes up the promise yet once more, and repeats it with exquisite pathos: "*For yet a little while—how little, how little—and He that is coming shall come, and shall not tarry*" (x. 37). Can it be that nineteen centuries were to be included in our Lord's "little while," or has He forgotten His word, we ask? And the apostle Peter answers: "But, beloved, be not ignorant of this one thing, that one day is with the Lord as a thousand years, and a thousand years as one day. The Lord is not slack concerning His promise" (2 Pet. iii. 8, 9). If those to whom these words were written could not comprehend them, we can do so in the light of accomplished time. Christ's resurrection is the miniature of that of His Church, both in circumstance and in time. It is written in the prophet Hosea: "*After two days will He revive us; in the third day He will raise us up, and we shall live in His sight*" (vi. 2). Our Lord's two days in the tomb are but a brief of the Church's two millenniums under humiliation and mortality; as also an epitome of Israel's two millenniums of rejection and cutting-off. But with Him we expect that, on the third day, God will raise us both up, and we shall live in His sight. Thus the "little while" that covered the two days of our Saviour's burial stretches across the two millennial days of the Church's militant state. But, measured on the scale of eternity, "how little, how little," is the time of waiting until we see Him again! This is an illustration of the prophetic perspective which belongs to many portions of Scripture, and it shows how God has provided for the raising and carrying forward of our vision to the one coming in which all others culminate.

Other examples equally striking might be cited; as, for instance, that prediction and transaction: "Verily I say unto you, There be some standing here which shall not taste of death till they see the Son of Man coming in His kingdom. And after six days He was transfigured before them" (Matt. xvi. 28). A miniature rehearsal of His glorious coming was here exhibited, enacted upon a miniature scale of chronology,—"*after six days*"—and presenting in vivid epitome that sabbatic glory which is to dawn when the world's weary working days are over. And the scene remains for all time, not as a type simply, but as an actual first instalment, as St. Peter interprets it, "of the power and coming of our Lord Jesus Christ" (2 Pet. i. 16).

If we note the events that were predicted to precede and herald the second advent—the appearance of Antichrist and the widespread preaching of the gospel—we find the same successive fulfilments, and the same consequent quickening of expectation. "Little children," writes John, "it is the last time: as we have heard that Antichrist shall come, even now are there many antichrists; whereby we know that it is the last time" (1 John ii. 18). These to which he refers were but incipient antichrists, feeble prototypes of that which was to follow; but their presence was enough to bring the end of the age and the return of Christ into vivid expectation. A few centuries later we find the Church, with St. Paul's Thessalonian prediction in its hands,—"For that day shall not come except there come a falling away first, and that Man of Sin be revealed,"—watching the impending fall of the Roman Empire, and expecting to see that Wicked One emerge from its ruins; since it was an apostolic tradition that the empire was the hindering power that must be taken out of the way before he could be revealed.[6]

---

[6] "We are now in the end and consummation of the world, the fatal time of Antichrist is at hand."—*Cyprian*, 3d century. "Who is he that letteth? Who but the Roman Empire? the

The anticipation cast a solemn gloom over the imagination of Christians; but it touched and kindled that gloom with the brightest hope, since it was known that, however terrible the monster, his appearance would be the precursor of the appearing of Christ, who would destroy him by the brightness of His coming. Thus was the advent-consummation brought again into vivid relief. The conception gathered from the prophetic Scriptures was that of a single man, the incarnation of diabolical wickedness, raging and reigning for three years and a half, and then destroyed by the lightning-flash of the epiphany. Such an idea was natural, and tended again to draw the *parousia* into startling proximity to the generation then living. But as centuries of fulfilling history began to throw their interpretation into prophecy, another conception inevitably emerged. Have we seen, over the shops, those curious changeable signs that present one name to the eye as we approach—which gradually dissolves in passing—and another name as we look back and read again? So with this prediction of Antichrist. To the early Church looking forward it seemed to foretell an individual Man of Sin, of three-years-and-six-months' reign. But when, out of the gloom and blood of the Middle Ages, the students of prophecy looked backward, they began to see what the apostolic Church could have hardly dreamed of,—a corporate Antichrist; the miniature Man of Sin, who had been expected, now magnified into a monstrous pseudo-Christian hierarchy; the Apocalyptic beast bestriding the centuries, red in tooth and claw with the blood of saints; his twelve hundred and sixty days' dominion expanded into as many years, constituting for the Church an era of unparalleled suffering and travail and tears; and as they saw and bore witness, once more there burst forth from the Church, from her prophets and reformers, such an advent-shout, "Behold He cometh," as centuries had not witnessed.[7] To say that the earlier interpreters were more likely to be correct

---

breaking up and dispersion of which among the ten kings shall bring on Antichrist. And then shall be revealed that Wicked One whom the Lord Jesus shall slay with the Spirit of His mouth."—*Tertullian*, 3d century. "This—the predicted Antichrist—shall come when the time of the Roman Empire shall be fulfilled and the consummation of the world approach."—*Lactantius*, 4th century.

[7] "Antichrist is already known throughout all the world. *Wherefore the day is not far off.*"—Latimer on 2 Thess. ii. 3, 1535. "O England, England, beware of Antichrist! Take heed he doth not deceive thee."—"*I trust our Redeemer's coming is at hand.*"—Bradford the Martyr, 1555. "I believe that all the signs which are to precede the last day have already

in their conception of Antichrist than we, upon whom the end of the age is dawning, is to say that those who gathered from our Lord's mysterious predictions—"*This generation shall not pass until,*" and "*there be some standing here who shall not taste of death till they see*"—the impression that the kingdom of God should immediately appear, more truly understood Him than we who have for our assistance the exegesis of providential events which eighteen centuries have been drawing out. It is enough to observe that, by a marvellous adjustment of prophecy and history, the watchers in the early Church, and in the modern Church alike, have found constant incitement to expectation.

To sum up our observations on this point: The long interval of apostasy and trial which lay before the Church ere the advent should arrive was both revealed and concealed in prophecy,—revealed even to the minutest circumstance and detail; yet in such hieroglyphic symbols[8] and chronology that it should remain graciously concealed until history should furnish the Rosetta Stone for its interpretation. The Apocalypse—which was to be the Church's *vade-mecum* through the long dark ages—was written in cipher, that it might not be comprehended prematurely, and thereby bring discouragement to the faithful; but events were commissioned to yield up the key to that cipher in due time, that the wise might understand and look up. To the first generation of Christians this guide-book seemed to show the Lord's coming near at hand; but when His coming was delayed, later generations could see that, according to the sure word of prophecy, it must

---

happened. The gospel is preached throughout the world: *the Son of perdition is revealed.*"—Luther, 1517.

[8] The miniature symbols are such as these: A beast for Antichrist, an enthroned harlot for the apostate Church; an exiled bride for the true Church, two candlesticks for faithful witnessing Churches. The miniature chronology accompanying these is the mystical number variously expressed,—"*time, times and half a time,*" "*forty and two months,*" "*a thousand two hundred and threescore days,*" etc. Since the symbols have been proved to stand for age-long realities, it seems incontestable that the chronology must stand for a correspondingly long period. Hence, since it covers the watching-time of the Church's history, it is always expressed enigmatically, that it might not be understood too early. The millennium, on the contrary, belonging to the time beyond the Lord's advent and the Church's waiting, is expressed in plain terms,—"*a thousand years.*"

have been so; and thus, instead of disappointment, there was a confirmation of Scripture that only gave new vigor to hope.

Holding that the Book of Revelation is the prophetic history of the Christian Church from our Lord's ascension to His return to usher in the millennium, we find that in itself it is a marvellous symbol. As given into the hand of the glorified Lamb to open, it is described as "*a book written within and on the back side, sealed with seven seals*" which seals represent the successive chapters of the Church's suffering and judgment throughout this dispensation.

Now, if by a "book" were meant the same thing which we describe by that word, the reader could turn the leaves through, and look onward at once to the last page to learn the issue. But here is a *roll*, sealed with seven seals, and only as history slowly unwinds that roll can its successive chapters be read. Hence mark the wondrous plan by which the reader's expectation is kept alert as it is unfolded. There are seven seals; under the seventh seal seven trumpets, and under the seventh trumpet seven vials. Now, the pondering and expectant Church reads chapter after chapter as the successive seals are loosed; and how anticipation kindles and glows upon the opening of the seventh, which is known to be the last! But, lo! under the seventh seal appear seven trumpets,—seven sub-divisions of the seventh chapter,—and so once more the expectation is checked, and then lifted and borne onward. But when angel after angel of judgment has sounded, and the seventh trumpet is ready to blow, what awed and solemn anticipation is once more roused, since it was under this that "*the mystery of God should be finished, as he hath declared to His servants the prophets*" (Rev. x. 7). But under the seventh trumpet again are seven vials,—seven chapters still of judgment under the last great chapter,—and once more the waiting Church looks onward; not in disappointment, but in hope, made stronger by experience, until the seventh vial is poured out, and the voice from heaven shall cry, "*It is done*" (Rev. xvi. 17).

As the Apocalypse is the Church's preordained history, so is this symbolic scroll the facsimile of that history. It is written within and without, just as the secular and sacred stand related to each other in their accomplishment; the history of the world and the history of the Church being the obverse and the reverse sides of the same transaction, the one permitted in the providence of

God to shape the other, and the other to interpret the one; and these two moving together as time unwinds the scroll of prearranged events. But what chapters within chapters! What fulfilment opening out of fulfilment, all alluring and onleading the hope towards that one divine event for which the whole creation groans! We remember sailing over a beautiful lake in Switzerland, journeying to the village that lay at its opposite end. Again and again, as the encircling hills shut in about us, the further shore seemed close at hand, and our destination nearly reached. But, rounding a projecting point, the aspect would change, the mountains would part once more, and another broad expanse of water would lie stretched out before us. Thus, by a singular peculiarity of the landscape, the journey's end seemed always imminent, and yet constantly receding. It was striking to observe how this feature of the journey affected the voyagers. Not a passenger was found at the ship's stern gazing backward. Every one was on the lookout. All eyes were bent forward in eager expectation, till at last the destined harbor was reached. Now all the commands and promises of Christ put us on the outlook, and every great juncture of fulfilling history sets us watching to discern whether the day-dawn is not approaching, whether the eternal hills are not closing in to bring the end of the age. The impulse which inspires us to watch, to expect, to be ready to disembark, however vain it may seem to men, has both the authority of God's word and the admonitions of all the history of the Church for its support. And, more than this, while none can know the day or the hour of the advent, we carry with us a chart of the Church's history to tell us approximately where in our stormy and perilous voyage we are. Its weird, mysterious pages contain the whole map and delineation of the Church's career from the ascension to the return of the Lord; but it was left for time to break the seals of this book and to discover its meaning. This it has been doing; and as, corresponding to this chart, headland after headland of the prophetic history has been descried, these have been recognized by the students who have been searching diligently what and what manner of time the Spirit did signify in penning this prophecy; and, though they have read no announcement of day or hour upon them, they have found them displaying the same cautionary signal with which the Church started: "*Behold, I come quickly: hold fast that which thou hast, that no man take thy crown*" (Rev. iii. 11). It is a warning startling enough to indicate that, though we know not how near the end of the age we may be, yet we are nearing it.

"Let your loins be girded about and your lights burning," therefore. There is enough of certainty in this subject to feed the lamp of our faith; and enough of uncertainty to make us very careful and solicitous lest when the Bridegroom comes we be found among the foolish virgins, saying, "Our lamps are gone out."

The chief point is, that this hope have a living and abiding place in our affections and our thoughts. "Thought," says a Christian father, "is the sleepless lamp of the soul." It is a lamp, indeed, that burns with varying brightness,—flaming up in moments of intense study and utterance, and dying down in sleep till there is only the pale glimmer that remains in dreams. But it is a lamp that is never really quenched; for however profound the slumber, it only requires a word to wake us, and to bring all our mental powers into instant activity. Thus must it be with the holy lamp of watchfulness,—always trimmed and burning, but not of necessity always shining in full strength. That is to say, we need not be every moment thinking of Christ's return, talking of it, and preaching it. There should be ever in our hearts the calm certainty and the sober hope that keep us ready for this event at any moment. But this hope should rather minister to us than be ministered to by us. Instead of perpetually dwelling on it and reiterating it, we should be lighted by it in our busy toil of gathering the guests for the marriage feast, and doing the work which our absent Lord has committed to us. Ready always to give to every man that asketh a reason for the hope that is in us, we should yet show the value of our lamp by the holy service into which it guides our feet, and the diligent piety which it makes visible in our lives.

III.
THE POWER OF HIS COMING.

CHRIST is not only coming in power at the last day, but the power of His coming is to be constantly operating in the present day. As God has appointed the moon to lift the tide by its attraction, that it may flood and fill all the indentures of the coast, so has He ordained this great event of Christ's *parousia* to draw up the faith and hope and love of the Church, when these have ebbed towards the world. If the philosopher is counted to have embodied the highest practical wisdom in his maxim, "Hitch your wagon to a star," can we question the efficacy of the divine method which has fastened all our hopes to "*the Bright and Morning Star*"? For, indisputably, the chief motive by which duties, obligations, aspirations, and attainments are determined in the New Testament is this, the ever-imminent return of the Lord from heaven. Therefore even the highest commendation that could be put upon a primitive church—"*ye come behind in no gift*"—was not so high that this crown could be omitted from it, "*waiting for the coming of our Lord Jesus Christ*" (1 Cor. i. 7). Such a tribute sounds strange to the Church of to-day, because she has so much accustomed herself to steer by the compass of her creed, instead of by the star of her hope; and to measure her position by the dead-reckoning of ecclesiastical history, instead of determining it by observation of those heavenly lights which God has given to rule the day and to rule the night. Yet here is a motive so transcendently powerful that, were it taken away, the Church would lose her upward gravitation.[9]

It is easy to say that absorption in the state of glory tends to render us careless concerning the serious claims of the state of humiliation. But we believe that quite the contrary is true. For our present not only makes our future, but is made by it; and that Christian alone can live well in the life that now is, who lives much in the life that is to come. As one has well written: "Only from the point of view of eschatology can we understand aright the

---

[9] "All the Apostolic exhortations and consolations are so closely connected with the prospect of the personal return of the Lord, that whoever contradicts this last, thereby takes away the roof and cornice from the structure of Apostolic Theology."—Van Oosterzee.

problems of the human life; for only when we recognize what is the *final* aim of life and being can we also set forth the goal to all the efforts of man. Therefore it has been said from an early period, *Respice finem.*"

Do we apprehend the total change of outlook which Christ has effected for the believer by His redemption, transforming a "*fearful looking-for of judgment*" into a joyful "*looking for that blessed hope*"? A sinner cannot look upward if he realizes his doom; a saint cannot look downward if he realizes his destiny. How deplorably, therefore, do they lower the standard of redemption who, by substituting *thanatology* for eschatology, fix our anticipations upon our departure through the gates of the grave, instead of lifting them to Christ's return through the gates of glory. If we make Death our hope, let us not be surprised if others learn to make him their hero.[10]

What, let us ask, are the attainments of the Christian life most insisted on in Scripture, and yet the most difficult to achieve, and how does the hope of Christ's personal return affect them?

Unworldliness, in the midst of the present evil world!—there is nothing which so powerfully promotes it as the realization that He whose servants we are may appear at any moment to reckon with us, and take us out of this world. Why is it that so many Christians make Death their executor, leaving thousands and millions to be dispensed by his bony fingers? Because they are exitists, rather than adventists; their going, and not Christ's coming, being the goal towards which they calculate. Therefore, if they die their wealth can stay behind: their covetousness can still survive and reap post-mortem usury. Living men, transporting their riches in daily installments into the world to come; or dead men remitting back their fortunes into this world, and still fingering the interest thereof in mortuary incomes,—here are the two ideals: and our Lord has plainly indicated which should be the Christian's in His saying, "Lay not up for yourselves treasures on earth; but lay up for yourselves

---

[10] Professor Duncan, commenting on the famous book of Carlyle, exclaims: "Hero-worship! Ah, well! he and I have to meet a strange hero yet— Θάνατος —the greatest that I know of *next to Him who overcame him.*" Let us look to it that by our death-homage, expressed in such mortuary poetry as,

"Death is the crown of life, . . .
Death gives us more than was in Eden lost,
The King of Terrors is the Prince of Peace,"

we do not take the crown from the head of the greater and place it on the head of the less.

treasures in heaven." And can there be any doubt that, if the position to which we have been called and raised by Christ's enthronement were really occupied and exulted in by us,—"*For our citizenship is in heaven, from whence also we look for the Saviour*"—the achievement of making heavenly investments would be easy and inevitable, and the grip of avarice be unclasped from the purse-strings of multitudes of Christians? The old nature is not sufficient for itself; and as truly as "the expulsive power of a new affection" is needed to overcome the heart-contraction of self-love, so truly is the uplifting power of a new hope required to break that purse-contraction of self-enrichment which is now the greatest obstacle to the evangelization of the world. The logic is inevitable; if we are citizens of heaven, we are "strangers and pilgrims in the earth;" and every rational instinct will lead us to make our investments where we hold our residence.

Not less difficult to overcome is that worldly-mindedness which seeks a present reward and a present glory. "*But it shall not be so among you,*" is the decisive rebuke of our Lord to such aspirations. But how not? By the vision of a millennial crown and throne, the heart is reconciled to a present cross and humiliation. "We have forsaken all and followed Thee; what shall we have, therefore?" "Ye that have followed Me*, in the regeneration, when the Son of man shall sit in the throne of His glory,* ye also shall sit upon twelve thrones judging the twelve tribes of Israel" (Matt. xix. 28). A dispensation of reproach for the Church cannot be perpetual; neither can a dispensation of glory be premature. The disciple must wait; but, in waiting for the reign of Immanuel, he is waiting for his own reign as heir-apparent to a crown of glory. Let us not, through a false humility, reject the doctrine of rewards, which Scripture so strongly emphasizes. But when and where? are the all-important questions. Constantly do we hear it said of one deceased, "He has gone to his reward." But, from the testimony of the Word, tell us where the believer is directed to look for his recompense at death? He is taught to aspire to a crown. But we are not to infer, because it is said, "Be thou faithful unto death,"—that is, up to the point of suffering martyrdom for Me,—"and I will give thee a crown of life," that our dying day is our crowning day, and that St. Sepulchre has been especially commissioned to preside at our coronation. To those who share Christ's travail and sorrow in the present life, for the rescuing of souls, a coronet of joy is promised. And when? "For what is our hope, or joy, or crown of rejoicing? Are not even ye *in the presence of our Lord Jesus Christ at His coming?*" (1 Thess. ii. 19.) To those who have chosen the portion of suffering with Christ in this world, as a little flock, it is written: "*And when the Chief Shepherd shall appear,* ye shall receive a crown of glory that fadeth not away" (1 Peter v. 4). To the steadfast soldier, who has fought the good fight, and finished his course, and kept the faith, the assurance is: "Henceforth there is laid up for me a crown of righteousness, which the Lord the righteous judge shall give me *at that day;* and not to me only, but *unto all them also that love His appearing*" (2 Tim. iv. 8). Of that other crown—the fourth—the time of the bestowal is not mentioned: "Blessed is the man that endureth temptation; for when he hath been approved *he shall receive the crown of life,* which the Lord promised to them that love Him" (James i, 12, R. V.). But since it is the *corona vitæ,* it is evident that it will be given at Christ's advent, when forever "death is swallowed up in victory," and not at our decease, when for the time life is swallowed up in defeat. Most inspiring is this doctrine of an open and final award to Christian fidelity. Martyrs have grasped it from afar, and been upheld amid the flames; and we, who are not called to suffer like them, learn also to exult in it as that which shall bring our vindication against such as contemn us, because we run not with them to the same excess of riot in world-getting and gain-grasping. For there is a real choice of recompense. Let no one say that this world has nothing to give the Christian; it has. Three times our Lord pronounces that solemn sentence concerning religious man-pleasers, "Verily I say unto you, they have their reward." The preëminent question is, whether there is power enough in the Redeemer's proffer, "*Behold, I come quickly, and My reward is with Me, to give to every man according as his work shall be,*" to disenchant the heart from this temporal and sordid recompense? Only when we realize our calling as the sons of God, "begotten again unto a lively hope," and made heirs of a reserved inheritance, can it be so. "The servant abideth not in the house forever;" and if we are only such, we shall demand day-wages, even as "the hireling looketh for the reward of his work." But "the son abideth ever," and therefore can "both hope and quietly wait" the final award of the inheritance.

If we turn from the perils of worldly-minded Christians to the trials of serious saints, we find the advent-hope serving the same end. Unless one is completely in the spell of a delusive optimism, he must often be appalled in contemplating the condition of the world. A thousand millions of the race still strangers to any form of Christianity; two thirds of nominal Christendom lapsed into an apostasy hardly better than paganism; and of the remaining third, only a meagre proportion really spiritual disciples! Without, the whole world lying in the Wicked One; and within, perpetual corruptions of doctrine, constant estrangements from the faith, daily reprisals of the Prince of Darkness upon the domain of light! A heart-swoon, like that which fell upon holy Daniel at the river Ulai, must sometimes seize the thoughtful Christian in view of all this, from which only a vision of the Ancient of Days, coming in the clouds of heaven, can rouse him. As, amid the desperate corruptions of the Catholic Church just previous to the Reformation, we find some who, having abandoned all hope from prelates and councils, took the name of "*Expectants*" and simply waited, such must we become, if we would be saved from disheartenment. We must not only look forward to the deliverance of the Coming One, but sometimes take our seat with Him in His throne, and share His attitude and anticipation as He sits there, "*expecting till His foes be made His footstool.*"

Then for that great overshadowing woe of mortality and corruption, what is the cure but the coming of the Coming One? "Thou shalt be recompensed *at the resurrection of the just*" said our Lord, speaking concerning the good deed done to the poor. But, in the light of other Scriptures, we may say that there is no promise that has so general an application. If death be the payment of the debt of nature, the first resurrection, at our Lord's appearing, will be the full repayment of the debt of grace. For this event will give us back all that we have lost: our friends in Christ, looking and speaking as they were wont; our inheritance in an earth renewed and glorified; and the temple of our body, no longer a house divided against itself through the conflict of sin, but raised up and re-dedicated with surpassing glory. Christ's redemption is not a compromise with Death, but a reimbursement for all of which he has robbed us,—a full refunding, exacted by the lawsuit of the atonement, of our defrauded inheritance. "I shall go to him, but he shall not return to me," was all that the broken-hearted David could utter concerning his dead child. But we who look for a Saviour can say more than this, since "them also which sleep in Jesus *will God bring with Him.*" What a beautiful, prophetic suggestion there is for us in that record of the Bethany feast which immediately follows the story of the raising of Lazarus: "*But Lazarus, which had been dead, whom He raised from the dead, was one of them that sat at the table with Him*" (John xii. I, 2). Often, in our advent anticipations, have we dreamed of the arrival of the long-looked-for consummation, and of our beloved dead suddenly reappearing, taking the vacant chair at the table, greeting us with the old familiar look, and speaking to us in the old familiar tones. If but a dream, this certainly is true: that the *parousia* will bring a real restoration, not simply a transfer into some strange society of shadows and spirits. Many seem to take pride in death, since they have learned to call it their *dies natalis*; but we confess that we are ashamed to die, rather than proud, since we know that in this event we shall have reached the pay-day of sin's wages.[11] Praised indeed be Immanuel, that dying now means our departing to be with Christ; but, nevertheless, it is a *return* for which we now wait,—His return, and our return with Him. Therefore has the Holy Ghost drawn for us that magnificent vision of the Lord Himself descending from heaven with a shout; and then, for the Church of all ages, is added the injunction: "Wherefore comfort one another with these words" (1 Thess. iv. 18).

"*Thine eyes shall see the King in His beauty: they shall behold a land of far distances*" (Isa. xxxiii. 17). Blessed is it if we are so long-sighted as to catch glimpses of that better country, amid the trial and turmoil of this; but doubly blessed, if we can look down upon this country through the far-reaching vistas of that, viewing the present life from the exalted stand-point of our Redeemer's throne. And this is permitted us. For there are what we may call spiritual rehearsals of the advent rapture, in which, like Paul, we are "caught up into Paradise" and hear unspeakable words. Let those bear witness who have proved it,—and there are such,—how utterly the whole scene of life has been changed in such moments. "Like Philip, I was caught away by the Spirit," writes one, "and was found, not at Azotus, but in the advent cloud, seated with my Lord in the chariot of His descending glory. A fire devoured before

---

[11] "For my own part, I must confess to you, that death, as death, appeareth to me as an enemy, and my nature doth abhor and fear it. But the thoughts of the coming of the Lord are most sweet and joyful to me; so that, if I were but sure that I should live to see it, and that the trumpet should sound, and the dead should rise, and the Lord appear before the period of my age, it would be the joyfulest tidings to me in the world. Oh that I might see His kingdom come! "—Richard Baxter.

Him, and it was very tempestuous round about Him. I heard Him call to the heavens from above, and to the earth, that He might judge His people, saying, 'Gather my saints together unto Me, those that have made a covenant with Me by sacrifice.' And as His redeemed ones came flying to Him, 'as a cloud, and as the doves to their windows,' from every tribe and kindred of earth, I beheld such as had been left behind. What wringing of hands there was among those who had loved gold supremely in a world which God so loved as to give His only Son for its redemption! What blanched faces upon those who had fared sumptuously and lived deliciously amid a starving and perishing race! Many of them who did so seemed to have worn the name of Christians; for, as I listened, I could hear a mighty wail borne up from them towards the descending Judge: 'Lord, Lord, have we not prophesied in Thy name? and in Thy name cast out devils? and in Thy name done many wonderful works?' But He only answered them: 'I never knew you: depart from Me, ye that work iniquity.' Whether in the body or out of the body when this transport was upon me, I cannot tell. But never since it occurred has the world been the same to me; nor can I think of its wealth, its luxury, its ease, its honors, without an instant prayer to be delivered from making these my gods."

Such "instant prayer" we may all well learn to offer, in the midst of our necessary work constantly sending up ejaculatory petitions that we may be delivered from the present evil world, so that, when our Lord appears in the clouds of heaven, we may bound towards Him by a resistless attraction, and be forever with Him.[12] Nothing can compensate for their loss who have eliminated this advent-hope from their creed. One love conquers another; and only by tasting "the powers of the world to come" can there be wrought in us a radical and enduring distaste for the vanities of the world that now is. Well, therefore, has one written concerning this hope, that, "of the life of watchfulness, patience, and heavenly-mindedness, it is the soul and power; and history makes abundantly manifest that, where this prospect has temporarily receded in the Christian consciousness, the spiritual life also has declined. One may confidently say that to a healthy Christian life '*etwas*

---

[12] "*O Almighty God, grant that those necessary works wherein we are engaged, whether in the affairs of Thy Church or of this world, may not prevail to hinder us; but that, at the appearing and advent of Thy Son, we may hasten with joy to meet Him, who liveth and reigneth with Thee and the Holy Ghost, ever one God, world without end. Amen.*"

Apocalyptisches"—something apocalyptical—also belongs; and that obligation to observe the signs of the times cannot possibly be fulfilled so long as the question as to the final whither has not, at least in principle, received an answer."

IV.
THE PROGRAMME OF REDEMPTION.

IT is remarkable to observe that the first council of the Christian Church ever convened should have outlined the whole scheme of redemption from Pentecost to the consummation of the ages. And whatever we may hold as to the binding authority of later councils, we must accept the deliverances of this at Jerusalem as final, since from the testimony of inspired Scripture we know that the Spirit so truly presided and guided in the assembly that in publishing its decisions it was written, "*It seemed good to the Holy Ghost and to us*" (Acts xv. 28). Jesus Christ is the Architect of the ages. Not only "all things were made by Him"—all worlds and systems of the material universe—but all the dispensations were planned and predestined by Him: "By whom also He made the ages" (Heb. i. 2). His Church was not set upon her course until a complete programme of her mission had been placed in her hands, the working-plan by which all her operations were to be directed. "*Known unto God are all His works from the beginning of the world*" (Acts xv. 18) is the significant declaration which accompanies the publication of this programme. And, instead of being day-laborers working in ignorance, God would have us, as laborers together with Him, to understand the entire divine scheme by which our efforts are to be directed, that we may be saved alike from presumption and from despair.

"*Simeon hath declared how God at the first did visit the Gentiles to take out of them a people for His name*" (Acts xv. 14). Here is the first act of the great programme. Because of the citation from the Old Testament which immediately follows—"And to this agree the words of the prophets, as it is written: After this I will return, and will build again the tabernacle of David which is fallen down"—it has been inferred that this Gentile outgathering and the tabernacle upbuilding mean the same thing; in other words, that the rearing of the tabernacle of David is a figurative expression for the building of the Church of Christ. By this superficial though not altogether unnatural explanation of the passage, the whole programme has been reduced to a single act, and the inference drawn that the preaching of the gospel in this dispensation is to issue in the conversion of "all the Gentiles."

But it is only necessary to observe three things in order to correct this misapprehension: First, that the citation here made from the closing chapter of the Book of Amos is clearly a prediction of the literal restoration of literal Israel, and their reinhabitance of their land; for the words quoted are part of a passage which ends with this decisive language: "*And I will plant them upon their land, and they shall no more be pulled up out of their land which I have given them, saith the Lord thy God*" (Amos ix. 15). Observe again that in making this citation the Holy Ghost inserts the words, not found in the original text, "*After this I will return*" and will build again, thus making the restoration of the Davidic tabernacle subsequent to the gathering out of the Church from the Gentiles, and connecting it directly with the personal return of the Lord. And, lastly, we are to notice that in announcing this election from among the Gentiles, it is not added, "in this are fulfilled the words of the prophets," but "with this harmonize—συμφωνοῦσιν, *symphonize*—the words of the prophets." It is but saying that the parts of the great oratorio of redemption perfectly accord, though centuries lie between its different measures; and then, to show us *how* they accord, the Holy Spirit sounds all the octaves thereof with a single sweep, and lets us listen to their grand unison. This, then, is the programme of redemption by which we are to work in evangelizing the world:—

"*First*, God did visit the Gentiles to take out of them a people for His name. And to this agree the words of the prophets, as it is written:—

"*After this* I will return and will build again the tabernacle of David which is fallen down; and I will build again the ruins thereof and I will set it up:

"*In order that* the residue of men might seek after the Lord, and all the Gentiles upon whom My name is called, saith the Lord who doeth all these things."

The three great stages of redemption are thus outlined in their order.

The gathering of the Church is the first act, and this, having begun at Pentecost, is still going on. All the descriptions of it contained in Scripture mark it as elective. From the word of Christ to His first disciples, "I have out-chosen you out of the world," to the triumph-song of the saved heard by the seer in Patmos, "Thou hast redeemed us to God by Thy blood *out of* every kindred and tongue and people and nation," the Bride of Christ is always the *Ecclesia,* the called out. Nowhere is universal redemption predicted as the result of preaching the Gospel in this dispensation. If in the minds of those who are accustomed to speak of the world's conversion there is a violent revulsion from this saying, we remind them that we are simply affirming the truth of the doctrine of election, and its application to this entire age. Most tenderly and reverently would we handle this solemn mystery of the Sovereign Will. "Who has not known passion, cross, and travail of death," says Luther, "cannot treat of this theme without injury to man or enmity to God." But it is written in Scripture, and the verdict of the ages declares it true. For after eighteen centuries of Christian conquest the vast proportion of the world still "lieth in the Wicked One," and Christ's true Church is but a "little flock" in comparison. Only with pathetic sympathy for our fallen race in its ruin and helplessness can we contemplate this fact. And yet we must be reminded that all attempts to violate this decree by making the Church a multitudinous collection, instead of a gracious election, have only issued in apostasy. Sacramentarianism would take the world into the Church by instituting a baptized paganism instead of taking the Church out of the world by preaching spiritual regeneration; and behold the result in a half-heathenized Christendom. Latitudinarianism would make the Church coextensive with the world by preaching the gospel of universal salvation,—all men by nature the sons of God,—and thus, by crowding the Lord's house with "the children of the Wicked One," turn it into "the synagogue of Satan." Though it be in mystery, and sorrow and tears, we had best work on, therefore, by the divine schedule, preaching the gospel among all nations for a witness that we may gather out for Christ a chosen and sanctified people, calmly answering those who say that God's ways are partial with His own words: "When that which is perfect is come, then that which is in part shall be done away."

And yet, lest we should take too narrow a view of this theme, other considerations should not be overlooked. Christ is called "The Light of the World." The beams of sunlight both elect and irradiate; taking out here and there from muddy pool or acrid dead sea a pure, crystalline drop and lifting it heavenward; but also lighting and warming all the atmosphere by their radiance. So Christ, preached among the Gentiles, elects from them a holy flock, a regenerate Church; but besides this, He changes the moral climate of the world so that such noxious growths as cannibalism, slavery, polygamy, and infanticide disappear. These two results inevitably attend the proclamation of the gospel; regeneration saving some out of the world, and civilization putting something of Christianity into the world: but by neither process as now going on is the millennium destined to be ushered in.

Moreover, let us reflect that *an election is never an end in itself;* it is rather a means and preparation for some vastly larger accomplishment. The body of the elect is really Christ's army, gathered by a divine conscription from every kindred and people, that they may attend Him as He goes forth to His final conquest of the world. "And they that are with Him are called and elect and faithful" (Rev. xvii. 14). Of this, however, we shall speak later.

The second act of the divine programme now comes into view. "*After this I will return and build again the tabernacle of David which is fallen down.*" By Christ's personal coming in glory, the conversion and restoration of Israel are to be accomplished. The reader has only to compare this order with the redemption schedule drawn out in the eleventh of Romans to see how perfectly they agree. St. Paul, indeed, begins with the Jewish election, as St. James does with the Gentile election. And we must remember that the choosing out that is going on in this dispensation touches both: "not out of the Jews only,—but also out of the Gentiles" (Rom. ix. 24). But each apostle takes up the same succession of events; first the Gentile outgathering, and then the Hebrew regathering. The hardening of the Jews which we now behold is declared by Paul to continue "until *the fulness of the Gentiles* be come in. And so all Israel shall be saved. As it is written: There shall come out of Zion the Deliverer, and shall turn away ungodliness from Jacob" (Rom. xi. 25, 26). By the "fulness of the Gentiles" we understand the predestined number, the elect company gathered through the entire period of this dispensation to form the Bride of Christ.[13] When this number shall have been accomplished, then the conversion of Israel will occur and their national restoration to God's

---

[13] The word πλήρωμα—*fulness*—is used to signify a limited fulness as well as an unlimited: it may apply to the contents of the brimming cup dipped from the ocean as well as to all the waters of the ocean. "When *the fulness of time* was come, God sent forth his Son" (Gal. iv. 4). Here is meant the completion of a certain preordained period of time. So "the fulness of the Gentiles" we hold to mean the entire number of those to be gathered out of the Gentiles during the age. See use of the word also in Mark ii. 21.

favor. The two parts of the aged Simeon's prophecy are strictly consecutive: "A *light* to lighten the Gentiles and the *glory* of Thy people Israel" (Luke ii. 31, 32). The sun is the light of the earth, overspreading it with his beams and electing and drawing up from it the pure water-drops which form the clouds; but he is the glory of the heavens, being their very central and most illustrious orb. And so is Christ a light for revelation to the nations, exhibiting God to them in Himself who is "the brightness of His glory and the express image of His person," in order to win from them a chosen heritage. But He will be the supreme glory of His people Israel, when He shall at last be owned as their Messiah and reign in the midst of them as King.

These two stages of redemption—the Gentile election and the Hebrew restoration—are to be accomplished "in order" to a third, namely, "that the residue of men might seek after the Lord, and all the Gentiles upon whom my name is called."

The old priority still holds, so far as world-wide salvation is concerned: "To the Jew first and also to the Gentile." This order was inverted for a time by the rejection of Christ by His people; but when they shall turn unto Him and find mercy, it will be taken up again. It stands written in Scripture that "*all Israel shall be saved*," and just as plainly, that through that consummation "*all the Gentiles upon whom my name is called.*" Without enlarging upon the thought, what a profound hint of this does Paul give in the words of the same chapter concerning his rejected people: "Now if the fall of them be the riches of the world, and the diminishing of them the riches of the Gentiles, *how much more their fulness.*" "For if the casting away of them be the reconciling of the world, *what shall the receiving of them be but life from the dead?*" (Rom. xi. 12, 15.) "It is clear," says Lange, "that the apostle awaits a boundless effect of blessing on the world from the future conversion of Israel." Then shall the word of Joel concerning the effusion of the Spirit have a complete fulfilment, as it had a partial and prefigurative accomplishment on the day of Pentecost. For if we turn to the prophet we find it said: "And ye shall know that *I am in the midst of Israel*, and that I am the Lord your God and none else. *And it shall come to pass afterward that I will pour out my Spirit upon all flesh*" (Joel ii. 27, 28). And with this agree the words of Isaiah where he predicts the desolation of Zion as continuing "*till the Spirit be poured upon us from on high*" (Is. xxxii. 15). When the Lord shall shed forth the Holy

Ghost abundantly upon His covenant people, through them will come unspeakable blessing to the Gentiles.[14] The modern post-millennial interpretation completely deranges the programme of prophecy at this point by making redemption terminate with its first scene. "The end of the age," brought in by the second coming of Christ, misleadingly translated "the end of the world" in our common version, is supposed by many to close the probation of the race, winding up the present earthly scene, and bringing in the final judgment and the eternal state, instead of opening into the triumphs of the age to come. Is it possible that the first Christians could have had this idea? If so, how could they have so ardently desired, and earnestly looked for, the speedy return of the Lord, since His coming would end the work of Gentile ingathering, while as yet only a handful had been saved? On the contrary, take the words of Peter to the Jewish rejectors of Christ, and observe how clearly they teach the very opposite: "Repent ye therefore and turn again, that your sins may be blotted out, that so there may come seasons of refreshing from the presence of the Lord; and that he may send the Christ who hath been appointed for you, even Jesus whom the heaven must receive until the times of the restoration of all things" (Acts iii. 19-21, R. V.). Here we have, as constantly throughout Scripture, the repentance of Israel directly connected with the return of Christ from heaven, and their conversion and the Lord's appearing resulting, not in their cutting off from the presence of the Lord, but in times of "*refreshing from the presence of the Lord*;" not in the winding up of all things, but in the "*restoration of all things.*" Three acts of the divine programme appear again in this declaration of Peter,—the coming of Christ, the conversion of Israel, and universal redemption,—corresponding exactly with those revealed in the texts from James and Paul already considered.

How clearly it is thus seen that the final redemption of the world comes at last through the conversion and restoration of Israel, and the glorifying of the Church at our Lord's return! If it be said that this is a Jewish conception, borrowed from the Old Testament,[15] we will answer, "Yes, and reiterated and

---

[14] "A new life in the higher charismatic fulness of the Spirit shall extend from God's people to the nations of the world compared with which the previous life of the nations must be considered dead."—Auberlen.

[15] "It is certainly not without significance that the Old Testament throughout binds the fulfilment of the Divine kingdom to the land that was granted to Abraham, not by right of

more explicitly unfolded in the New Testament." For nowhere is the order of events so distinctly revealed as in the Acts and Epistles.

"Election, partial and opposed to universal redemption," has been the verdict of thousands who have replied against God, knowing little of the range of His eternal plan. "Election, gracious, and preparatory to universal redemption," is the discovery which a deep pondering of Holy Scripture reveals. The chosen nation, Israel, restored and made glorious on earth, with the Lord dwelling in the midst of her, and the elect Church transfigured with her risen Saviour,—these are His appointed agents, trained by long discipline and trial for bringing all peoples and tribes into obedience to God. As to the Gentile election, so to the Hebrew restoration, objectors may be reconciled when it appears that this, too, is instrumental and preparatory to world-wide salvation. "Arise, shine, for thy light is come, and the glory of the Lord is risen upon thee," is the summons which the long captive daughter of Zion shall hear, and then the blessed result: "*And the Gentiles shall come to thy light, and kings to the brightness of thy rising*" (Is. lx. 3). No dream of the world's conversion, however ardent, can surpass the glowing reality as depicted in the prophecy just quoted,—"The abundance of the sea," "The forces of the Gentiles," "The inhabitants of the isles," coming no longer by ones and twos, but in clouds! Only let us observe the order of their coming,—through restored and forgiven Israel,—that we may understand the Messianic prayers which are taught us in the Scripture to be the truest missionary prayers. To plead for the speedy return of the Lord is to plead for the speedy ingathering of the heathen; to pray for the peace of Jerusalem is to pray for the conversion of the Gentiles. How this comes out in the words of the sixty-seventh Psalm!—"God be merciful unto *us* and bless *us*, and cause His face to shine upon *us; that Thy way may be known upon earth, Thy saving health among all nations.*" The Jews have been in the shadow of God's averted countenance ever since they rejected His Anointed, and hid, as it were, their faces from Him. But when they shall repent and return to Him, He will turn His face again upon them in blessing. Then will redemption go forth unhindered and

---

nature, but by grace. The prophets know of no final completion of the Divine promises without the confirmation of this old promise of the eternal possession of the Holy Land."— Oehler, *Old Testament Theology*, i. p. 93.

without measure upon the Gentiles.[16] "Then shall the earth yield her increase, and God, even our own God, shall bless us, *and all the ends of the earth shall fear Him.*" Blessed time, when God's patient seeking after the Gentiles shall give place to a universal seeking of the Gentiles after God. "And the inhabitants of one city shall go to another, saying, Let us go speedily to pray before the Lord and to seek the Lord of Hosts. I will go also, yea, many people and strong nations shall come to seek the Lord of Hosts in Jerusalem, and to pray before the Lord" (Zech. viii. 21, 22). To those, therefore, who would dishearten us by declaring that missions to the heathen are a failure, and that, at the end of nineteen centuries of evangelization by the Church, there are a thousand million of earth's fourteen hundred millions who have not even named the name of Christ,—that "for every additional Christian, we have every year a hundred and eighty additional heathens or Moslems,"—our answer is, An exhortation to redoubled diligence in preaching the gospel to every creature, that we may thereby "hasten the day of God;" an invocation, "Even so come Lord Jesus;" and a prayer which we breathe out in the most fitting words of the old English burial service: "That it may please Thee *shortly to accomplish the number of Thine elect and to hasten Thy kingdom*, that we, with all those that are departed in the true faith of Thy holy name, may have our perfect consummation and bliss, both in body and soul, in Thy eternal and everlasting glory, through Jesus Christ our Lord. Amen."

---

[16] "Those beautiful questioning words of Isaiah about the Gentiles often occur to me: 'Who are these who fly as doves to their windows?'—a flock of doves speeding to their home, their ark of refuge. Noah's one dove, like the solitary Jewish Church, took refuge there from the wild waste of waters; but all kindreds, people, tongues, and nations shall fly to their stronghold in later times, their feathers of gold and their wings covered with silver, white and lovely though they have lain among the pots."—*Patience of Hope.*

V.
THE ENDS OF THE AGES.

THREE consecutive ends of ages come into view in the New Testament: First (Heb. ix. 26), "*Once in the end of the ages* hath he appeared to put away sin by the sacrifice of Himself,*" Christ's first coming, terminating the Jewish economy in the judgment and rejection of the house of Israel, and opening the door of grace to the Gentiles; second (Matt. xiii. 49), "*At the end of the age* the angels shall come forth and sever the wicked from among the just," Christ's second coming, attended by the first resurrection and the rapture of the Church, terminating the dispensation of grace in the judgment of apostate Christendom, restoring Israel, and introducing the millennium; third (1 Cor. xv. 24, R. V.), *"Then cometh the end,"* when He shall deliver up the kingdom to God even the Father," the close of the millennium, the resurrection of the rest of the dead, and the last judgment.

Observe with what dramatic solemnity each of these successive ages is brought to a close. On the cross of Golgotha, amid the rending of the temple veil, the shock of earthquake, and the darkening of the sun, Christ ended the first with that mighty cry: "*It is finished*" (John xix. 30). Amid voices, and thunders and lightnings, and an earthquake, and the outpouring of the seventh vial, the present age is closed, a great voice out of the temple of heaven, from the throne, saying: "*It is done*" (Rev. xvi. 17). With the passing away of the first heaven and the first earth, and the abolishing of death and sorrow and crying and pain, the millennial age is brought to an end, He that sitteth on the throne saying: "*It is done*, I am Alpha and Omega, the beginning and the end" (Rev. xxi. 6).

What is called the post-millennial theory—the doctrine that Christ's return is at the end of the millennium instead of the beginning—maintains its position by telescoping the ages, running the second and third together, and so making their principal events to synchronize. It is agreed that *a* resurrection takes place at the advent of Christ. But pre-millennialists hold that this is "the first resurrection,"—the rising of the just,—and that a chiliad will elapse between it and the second resurrection, during which period Christ will reign over the earth with His glorified Church, and that therefore His coming must be pre-millennial. This might not appear to one whose eye is not trained by a diligent study of the Word to apprehend the perspective of prophecy. But will our readers follow us carefully, and see whether the position is not justified by an appeal to Scripture.

The following text we regard as having to do with three consecutive ages (1 Cor. xv. 22-29): "In Christ shall all be made alive. But every man in his own order: *Christ the first-fruits,*"—at the close of the Jewish dispensation,—"*afterward they that are Christ's at His coming*"—at the close of the present dispensation,—"*then cometh the end*"—at the close of the millennial dispensation. This last "end," however, is held by post-millenarians to mean the time of Christ's coming and the resurrection of all, both righteous and wicked; so that there is no considerable period between the advent and the final consummation.

But observe the significant adverbs "*afterwards*" and "*then*— ἔπειτα; εἶτα.[17] They are correlatives; and as we know that one describes an era of at least nearly nineteen hundred years, it is quite impossible to suppose that the other indicates no considerable period of time. And this is not all. Scripture is like a dissected map, whose scattered parts we must fit together if we would discover what is the divine pattern of the ages. And, turning to the Apocalypse, we find that it gives us the period and the events with which to fill up this disputed space between the resurrection of them that are Christ's at His coming and the end. For in its pages we have a vision of "*the first resurrection*"—that which all Scripture teaches us to connect with Christ's second advent—and then the statement that "*the rest of the dead lived not again until the thousand years were ended,*" and between these two, the glorified saints reigning with Christ a thousand years (Rev. xx. 4-6). If plain language may be plainly interpreted, this gives us the filling up of the outline revealed in Corinthians, and verifies the schedule of the ages with which we begin this chapter.

Moreover, if we observe the events which are connected with the "end" in the Corinthian prophecy, we see how clearly they define it. "Then cometh the end *when He shall deliver up the kingdom to God, even the Father*" (1 Cor.

---

[17] "By the words ἔπειτα and εἶτα two separate epochs are distinctly marked; and it is a violation of all usage of terms to construe them otherwise. The interval of the first is stretching beyond 1,800 years; how many ages will intervene between the second and the third, who can tell?"—Kling.

xv. 24, R. V.). But on Christ's appearing at the close of the present age, He takes the kingdom from the Father. As Daniel sees One like unto the Son of man coming with the clouds of heaven, he beholds Him invested with kingship by the "Ancient of Days:" "*And there was given Him* dominion and glory and a kingdom, that all peoples and nations and languages should serve Him" (Dan. vii. 13, 14). Can our Lord's receiving the kingdom from the Father mean the same thing as His delivering up the kingdom to the Father?[18] In Revelation the representation is precisely the same. As the seventh angel sounds—the angel of the last trump under which the righteous dead are raised (1 Cor. xv. 52)—there are great voices in heaven saying: "The kingdom of this world is become the kingdom of our Lord and of His Christ;" and the response from the four and twenty elders is: "We give thee thanks, O Lord God Almighty, which art and wast and art to come,"—this is the title of the glorified Christ (i. 8),—"*because Thou hast taken to Thyself Thy great power and hast reigned.*" This certainly is Christ's assumption of the kingdom rather than His surrender of it. Not only does He receive the kingdom at His advent, but, according to this same prophecy of Daniel, His redeemed people share its reign and judgment with Him: "And the time came that *the saints possessed the kingdom*" (Daniel vii. 22). But this time is shown in Revelation to extend from the first resurrection to the second resurrection: "Blessed and holy is he that hath part in the first resurrection: on such the second death hath no power; but they shall be priests of God and of Christ, *and shall reign with Him a thousand years*" (Rev. xx. 6). Observe, again, that the last end which we are considering is "the end . . . *when He shall have put down all rule and authority and power.*" Does He not begin this work at His advent, when He destroys Antichrist, and all his vast array of allied wickedness, by the brightness of His coming? "*For He must reign till He hath put all enemies under His feet.*" But at His coming for the first resurrection, He finds His enemies unsubdued, the nations angry, the apostasy ripe for judgment. This cannot be the time of the

---

[18] "Is the object of Christ's coming to *surrender* the kingdom to the Father, or does He come first of all to rightly *enter* upon it? Undoubtedly the latter. The appearing of Christ is at the same time the appearing of His Kingdom. This unquestioned, then it is clear that the return of Christ is rather for the purpose of assuming than assigning the kingdom, and therefore the parousia of Christ and the End of the World do not coincide, but on the contrary are separated from each other."—Luthardt, *Lehre von den Letzten Dingen*, p. 129.

completed subjection of His foes. "*The last enemy that shall be destroyed is death.*" Yet it is only at the end of the millennium, at the termination of the thousand years' reign of the saints, and after the white-throne judgment, that the announcements are heard: "And death and hell were cast into the lake of fire;" "*And there shall be no more death*" (Rev. xx. 14; xxi. 4). We find, therefore, an entire era of the conquest and reign of Immanuel and His saints between the resurrection at His glorious appearing and the end when He shall surrender His kingdom. These considerations would seem to establish conclusively the pre-millennial order of Christ's coming; but there are others.

The present age is everywhere set forth in Scripture as one of mingled darkness and light, towards the end of which the shadows rather deepen into judgment than break away before a triumphant millennial dawn. The parables of the kingdom, contained in the thirteenth chapter of Matthew, are decisive in their teaching. These parables are seven; and we hold that—like the seven prophetic pictures of the Apocalyptic churches—they portray the successive eras of the history of Christendom from the beginning of the dispensation to its close.[19] In them we have a vivid delineation of the trials and resistance which the kingdom of heaven was to encounter from the Adversary, from its first introduction into the world until the end of the age; and if, in their exposition, we are guided by the light which other Scriptures throw upon them, we seem to discover both a logical and a chronological order in the teaching which they set forth.

In the first parable, the seed is "the word of the kingdom." As it is sown, three parts fall into unfruitful soil, and only one part into good ground. Does not this harmonize with the universal experience of the preachers of the Gospel, from the day of our Lord's ministry until this present, that only the smaller fraction of their hearers give fruitful heed to the Word?

---

[19] The Epistles to the Seven Churches, besides describing what is undoubtedly historical, have so many allusions which are evidently figurative and mystical that there is the strongest reason for accepting the view advanced by Mede, one of the earliest Protestant Apocalyptic commentators, and received by many later expositors, that it was intended "that these seven churches should prophetically sample unto us a sevenfold temper and constitution of the whole Church according to the several ages thereof, answering the pattern of the churches named here."

In the second parable, we take the field that is really receptive, and into which good seed has been cast, and, lo! tares are found to have been sown therein by the Adversary, which now appear growing together with the wheat. This our Lord explains to mean the mingling of "the children of the Wicked One" with "the children of the kingdom." And is not this exactly what came to pass in the first stages of the apostasy, the bringing of unregenerated men into the Church of Christ and mixing them with true saints? With this second parable of the kingdom harmonizes most strikingly the second stage of prophetic Christian history as exhibited in the Church of Smyrna (Rev. ii. 9),—"I know the blasphemy of *them that say they are Jews and are not, but are of the synagogue of Satan;*" false professors personating the true, the children of the Wicked One palming themselves off as children of the kingdom (see Rom. ii. 28).

The third parable shows the result. The kingdom of heaven becomes a lofty and overshadowing world-church.[20] The mustard-seed springs up, but not according to its kind; from an herb it grows into a great tree, and the birds of the air that once sought to destroy the seed of the kingdom now lodge in its branches; the emperors and kings who had striven to uproot the pure Church find shelter in this secular Church, which, in its changed condition, overspreads the earth with marvellous rapidity. Let one read this parable in the light of the same representation as given by the prophets (Ezk. xxxi. 3-14, and Dan. iv. 10-19), and he can hardly conclude that our Lord intended herein to set forth a true spiritual growth of His Church. It is rather the Pergamos period of her development which the prophetico-historic interpreters have understood to be the era of the union of Church and State, wherein what was originally "not of this world" becomes a vast world-kingdom. The prophetic prefigurement in the Apocalypse is very striking,—Balaam conspiring with Balak, the prophet with the king, to seduce the children of Israel into idolatry (Rev. ii. 14),—even as, in the history of the Church, the bishops and the emperors by their ecclesiastical alliance paganized Christianity.

The fourth parable gives the result of this rank prosperity of the Church in the complete corruption of her life and doctrine: *"The kingdom of heaven is like unto leaven which a woman took and hid in three measures of meal till*

---

[20] "As the mustard-seed even changes its species, passing from an herb to a sort of tree, *so does the kingdom of heaven pass into the likeness of a great world-state.*"—Lange.

the whole was leavened." Let those who affirm that this parable signifies the gradual penetration and saving transformation of the whole world by the Gospel reflect that, in order to get this interpretation, they must give to leaven a directly opposite meaning from that which Scripture invariably assigns to it, since it is always employed in the Bible as a type of corruption, there being absolutely no exception to this usage in Old Testament or New.[21] Hear our Lord's admonition to "*take heed and beware of the leaven of the Pharisees and of the Sadducees,*" meaning thereby their false doctrines (Matt. xvi. 12). Listen to the exhortations of the apostle against "*the leaven of malice and wickedness*" (1 Cor. v. 8). Warning the Galatians of the doctrine of the Judaizers, he bids them remember that "*a little leaven leaveneth the whole lump*" (Gal. v. 9). Reproving the Corinthian Church for harboring fornicators, he uses the same phrase, and adds: "*Purge out, therefore, the old leaven, that ye may be a new lump, as ye are*"—according to your calling and profession—"*unleavened*" (1 Cor. v. 7). Comparing Scripture with Scripture,—the only method of interpreting difficult texts,—it seems clear that this parable of the leaven symbolizes the apostate Church, "which did corrupt the earth with her fornication" (Rev. xix. 2), and not the true Christianity, which was to transform the whole earth by the Gospel. The only instance where the use of leaven was commanded in Jewish worship affords a striking confirmation of this interpretation. Rigidly and repeatedly was its employment forbidden in the Passover service, because that service was foretypical of Christ, who should be without spot or blemish. But the wave-loaves of the feast of Pentecost were commanded to be "*baken with leaven*" (Lev. xxiii. 17); and Pentecost is believed to have been foretypical of the Church, as the Passover was of Christ; and its corruption by the leaven of false doctrine was thus possibly foreshadowed even in a Jewish rite and ceremony.

But could the kingdom of heaven be compared with an evil or corrupt thing? Not in its primitive and original condition certainly. But in its deteriorated state it might. "*Then* shall the kingdom of heaven be likened unto ten virgins: ... five of them were wise and *five were foolish*" (Matt. xxv. 1, 2). Here the kingdom of heaven, as it will be immediately previous to the coming

---

[21] Even the heathen attached this significance to it, as shown by the following sentence of Plutarch, as cited by Wetstein: "*Now leaven is both generated itself from corruption, and it corrupts the mass with which it is mingled.*"

of Christ, is compared with what is *semi-apostate*, according to the invariable representation of the mixed condition prevailing at that period. If, as we believe, the parable of the leaven belongs to the Middle Ages, when the Church was *completely apostate*, it is clearly reasonable that the kingdom should *then* be compared with leaven, which is the synonym of corruption. And can we fail to be struck with the exact correspondence between the fourth parable of the seven in Matthew and the fourth prophecy of the seven in the Apocalypse? As in the one a woman is seen hiding leaven in the meal, so in the other is pictured "*that woman Jezebel teaching and seducing Christ's servants to commit fornication, and to eat things sacrificed to idols*" (Rev. ii. 20); that is, the papacy disseminating false doctrine in the Church, and adulterating its worship with pagan rites and ceremonies.

Such we believe to be the interpretation of this much-disputed parable which Scripture compels, and we may add also, which history confirms.[22] For if one holds that here is a similitude of the transformation of the whole world by the Gospel, he can show no fulfilment in fact; since, after nearly twenty centuries, the vastly larger part of the world is still pagan, unchristian or antichristian. If the parable signifies the corruption of the whole prophetic earth by the leaven of paganized Christianity, history gives a perfect confirmation of it; since, just before the dawn of the Reformation, it was proudly boasted by the Roman hierarchy that all opposition had at last been silenced, and the entire Christian world brought into acquiescence with the Apostate Church.

Having uttered these four parables in the presence of the multitude, our Lord makes a significant break in His discourse and sends them away; then, entering into the house, He speaks the remaining three to His disciples. What do these last signify? An eminent commentator, Dr. Schaff, following a totally different exposition of the earlier parables from that we have indicated, when reaching the parable of the hid treasure remarks on the striking historical likeness which is presented to it in what occurred at the Reformation. We consider that this may be the intended prophetic reference. It is God's elect

---

[22] Some, who cannot admit that the parable of the leaven refers to the corruption of the Church, concede that it may bear this as a secondary meaning. Richter's House Bible says: "*The mixed degeneracy and sinfulness of the no longer apostolically pure Church which now extends itself is at the same time meant*"

people who are repeatedly called in Scripture His "peculiar treasure" (Ex. xix. 5; Ps. cxxv. 4, etc.). In "the field" where the kingdom of heaven has been so resisted and thwarted by the Adversary this treasure now lies hid out of sight. "The kingdom of God is as it were buried beneath the clods of false Christianity,—of superstition, human ordinances and ceremonies" (Roos). Is not this the Sardis period of the Church, nominal Christianity alone visible? "I know thy works, that thou hast a name that livest and art dead." But there is a hidden remnant:[23] *"A few names even in Sardis that have not defiled their garments."* At what cost of martyr-blood and of the selling of all—property, friends, and life—was this hidden treasure recovered, and what boundless joy resulted! So likewise of the sixth parable, that of the pearl. The sixth Church of the Apocalypse, Philadelphia, which has been held to be the Church of the Reformation, has this as its distinctive honor: "*Thou hast kept my Word.*" By the hand of such as Wiclif, and Luther, and Tyndal, who heard the command of God, "Buy the truth and sell it not," the priceless pearl of the Holy Scriptures, or, forsooth, that pearl of pearls, the doctrine of justification by faith,—long hidden from the people under the rubbish of the apostasy,—was again brought to light and held forth, at what countless cost of life and substance, but also amid what exultant rejoicing!

The seventh parable is most striking in its forecasting of the times in which we live: "Again the kingdom of heaven is like unto a net that was cast into the sea, and gathered of every kind"—ἐκ παντὸς γένους—"*out of every race.*" Here is the draw-net of world-wide missions; and the fact that our Lord interprets the parable as applying to the close of the dispensation shows how perfectly its teaching accords with His own prophecy that towards the end the Gospel of the kingdom should be preached among all nations. It will be seen thus that as the first parable, in which the Son of man is the sower, touches our Lord's first advent, so the seventh touches His second advent. And it is certainly natural to conclude—since seven is in Scripture the number of completeness—that the others span the entire interim. The result of this net-casting is, according to the

---

[23] "The kingdom of heaven is represented as having once more become invisible in the visible Church; as hid like a treasure, erst concealed in a most unlikely place, in the midst of worldly things. It appears as a treasure-trove—a free gift of grace—discovered by a person in a fortunate hour while he was engaged in digging: true Christianity, when again discovered, a subject of great joy."—Lange on *The Parable of the Hid Treasure.*

invariable teaching of Scripture, a mixed gathering, in which righteous and unrighteous are found together at last, awaiting the separation of judgment. Is there any likeness here to the seventh or Laodicean picture of the Church, "*Because thou art lukewarm*"? If we may credit the quaint suggestion of an expositor that "lukewarmness is the result of the mingling of extremes of cold and heat in the same vessel," there is. At all events, this picture agrees with the combined teaching of the Scriptures concerning the close of the dispensation. It will be an age of mingled zeal and formalism; evangelical fervor carrying the servants of Christ to the ends of the earth proclaiming the everlasting Gospel, and abounding iniquity causing the love of many to wax cold. The last period, however, does not seem to be the period of the widest and completest apostasy of the Church, as some would teach. That era is the middle era, when the whole lump was leavened; subsequently to this, there is a partial and glorious recovery. This is for our joy, amid all in the outlook which is for our admonition. The sailors on the Southern Sea sing, "*Midnight is past, the cross begins to bend.*" And we, as voyagers through these troubled ages, in which are the sea and the waves roaring, and men's hearts failing them for fear, may sing, "Midnight is past." Let not those who are looking for the millennium instead of Christ paint a future for the Church of untinged brightness; let not those who are looking for Antichrist instead of Christ picture a future for the Church of unmitigated blackness: for neither representation is true to prophecy. "Watchman, what of the night? The Watchman said, "*The morning; cometh and also the night.*"

Trace through whatever line we will, we find the same condition at the end of the dispensation. If from the seed-time of the world we look on to the reaping-time, we find the wheat and the tares, the children of the kingdom and the children of the Wicked One, growing together until the harvest; then separated each for his destiny: "*So shall it be at the end of the age*" (Matt. xiii. 40).

If we watch with joy the ingatherings of the Gospel net as it sweeps through the nations, we find that, when it is full and drawn to the shore, the good are gathered into vessels, but the bad are cast away: "*So shall it be at the end of the age*" (Matt. xiii. 49).

If we listen to our Lord's great eschatological discourse, we hear prediction after prediction of wars, and famines, and pestilences, persecutions, and apostasies, and false christs, together with a world-wide preaching of the

Gospel for a witness; but instead of any gleam of millennial glory in the solemn prophecy, we find it culminating in such a time "as it was in the days of Noah." And all this is our Saviour's answer to the question, "What shall be the sign of Thy coming and of *the end of the age*?" (Matt. xxiv. 3.)

If we question the Scriptures concerning the characteristics of the last time as set forth by the apostles, we are told that these shall be "*perilous times*" (2 Tim. iii. 1),—times in which "some shall depart from the faith, giving heed to seducing spirits and doctrines of demons, speaking lies in hypocrisy, having their conscience seared with a hot iron, forbidding to marry, and commanding to abstain from meats" (1 Tim. iv. 1-3); that whereas in primitive days Christians lived in sober expectation of the Lord's return, "there shall come in the last days scoffers, walking after their own lusts, and saying, Where is the sign of His coming?" (2 Pet. iii. 3, 4.)

If we inquire concerning the dispensation as a whole, we learn that the purpose of our Redeemer's work was, not that He might transform this into a present golden age, but "that He might deliver us from *this present evil age*" (Gal. i. 4); not that He might conform this age to us, but that we should "*be not conformed to this age*" (Rom. xii. 2). Such statements suggestively indicate that it is not the divine purpose to millennialize the present dispensation, but rather to call out from it a holy Church, a separated people.

For what, moreover, are the age-long characteristics as revealed in Scripture? Paul, in teaching the Thessalonians concerning the second coming of Christ, admonishes them that, before that day could arrive, there must first come a falling away and a revelation of the man of sin. And he tells them that this apostasy had even then begun,—"the mystery of iniquity doth already work,"—and that out of it "that Wicked" would be revealed, "whom the Lord shall consume with the spirit of His mouth, and shall destroy with the brightness of His coming." Here is a demonstration from Scripture that the predicted apostasy would stretch across the entire age from the days of Christ's immediate apostles to the day of His second advent, when in its consummated development it would confront the descending Judge and meet its doom. Is it, then, a ripe millennium that welcomes the returning Lord at His epiphany, or a ripe apostasy? Let him that readeth understand.

Again, since God's ancient people Israel are everywhere represented in Scripture as having a blessed share in the triumphs and joys of the millennial glory, let us ask what their condition is to be in this dispensation. In our Lord's great prophecy concerning His second coming and the end of the age, He answers this question conclusively. He describes in graphic outlines the destruction of Jerusalem, with the events preceding and portending it. After using language that can only apply to that appalling event,—"Pray ye that your flight be not in the winter,"—He adds, "*For there shall be great tribulation, such as was not since the beginning of the world to this time,—no, nor ever shall be*" (Matt. xxiv. 20, 21). How long shall this tribulation continue? Until Christ's second coming. For our Lord declares that "*immediately after the tribulation of those days*" the signs of the advent shall be witnessed, when "they shall see the Son of man coming in the clouds of heaven with power and great glory" (xxiv. 30). So closely are these two events connected in the prediction that some have argued that Christ's advent must have actually occurred at the destruction of Jerusalem, in a spiritual or providential sense. But a careful examination of the language employed proves beyond question that it is a literal coming that is here described, and that a literal immediateness after the great tribulation is affirmed by the word, εὐθέως "immediately." If we turn to Luke's Gospel, however, and read his parallel report of our Lord's words, all becomes plain (Luke xxi. 23-27). For he makes the tribulation to include the dispersion of the Jews among all nations, and the treading down of their Holy City by the Gentiles, "*until the times of the Gentiles be fulfilled.*" In other words, the great tribulation covers the entire age from Zion's captivity to Messiah's coming. To say that the millennium is to precede Christ's advent, therefore, is to affirm the possibility of putting that era of unparalleled blessing into the same period which is occupied by this unequalled tribulation; in other words, it is to identify and synchronize the golden age of Israel's triumph with the gloomy age of Israel's trouble. This cannot be. For we see in prophecy that the great apostasy and the great tribulation so far preempt the present dispensation, that the Church's millennium and Israel's millennium are alike crowded out, and there is found no place for them, till the Lord descends in glory to destroy Antichrist and restore Israel.

PART II.

FORFEITED.

"Our looking at Christ's coming as at a distance is the cause of all those irregularities which render the thought of it terrible to us."

MATTHEW HENRY.

"Chiliasm disappeared in proportion as Roman Papal Catholicism advanced. The Papacy took to itself as a robber, that glory which is an object of hope, and can only be reached by the obedience and humility of the cross. When the Church became a harlot she ceased to be a Bride who goes forth to meet her Bridegroom, and thus Chiliasm disappeared."

AUBERLEN.

"In plucking up the faith of Christ's coming Satan aims directly at the throat of the Church. For to what end did Christ die and rise again, but that along with Himself he might some day redeem us from death, and gather us into eternal life?"

CALVIN.

I.
HEAVENLY CITIZENSHIP.

A MAN'S dwelling in one country, and holding citizenship in another and far remote country, is not an unknown circumstance. In such a case, we may have the singular anomaly of one being most a stranger in the land in which he is present, and most at home in the land from which he is absent. Our blessed Lord was the first perfectly to realize this idea respecting the heavenly country. For He speaks of Himself as "He that came down from heaven, even the Son of man who is in heaven." So truly a citizen of the other world was He that even while walking with men and talking with men He regarded Himself as there, not here. And this saying of His occurs in that discourse where, with an emphatic "verily, verily," He declares that "except a man be *born from above* he cannot see the kingdom of God."

Here is the key to the whole mystery. As the only begotten of the Father, Christ's native country was above; and during all the days of His flesh He neither relinquished His heavenly citizenship nor acquired an earthly residence. "Blessed be the Lord God of Israel: for He hath *visited* and redeemed His people," is a significant note in the prophecy of His birth. And four times in the Gospels is our Lord's advent to earth spoken of as a visit. But it was a visit which never for a moment looked toward a permanent abiding. At His birth He was laid in a borrowed manger, because there was no room for Him in the inn; at His burial He was laid in a borrowed tomb, because He owned no foot of earth; and between the cradle and the grave was a sojourn in which "the Son of man had not where to lay His head." The mountain top whither He constantly withdrew to commune with His Father was the nearest to His home. And hence there is a strange, pathetic meaning in that saying, "And every man went unto his own house; Jesus went unto the Mount of Olives."

Now, as it was with the Lord, so it is to be with His disciples. "*For our citizenship is in heaven,*" says the apostle. Herein is the saying of Lady Powerscourt true: "The Christian is not one who looks up from earth to heaven, but one who looks down from heaven to earth." A celestial nativity implies a celestial residence; and with a certain divine condescension may the

Christian contemplate the sordid, self-seeking children of this present evil age and say, with his Lord: "Ye are from beneath; I am from above: ye are of this world; I am not of this world." Let us be admonished, however, that to say this truly and to live it really may subject us to the experience indicated by the apostle: "Therefore the world knoweth us not because it knew Him not." There is a certain quaint beauty in the apology which an old reformer made for the hard treatment which he and his friends received from the men of this world. "Why, brethren," he would say, "they do not understand court manners or the etiquette of heaven, never having been in that country from whence we come; therefore it is that our ways seem strange to them." Would that in the Christians of to-day celestial traits were so conspicuous as to occasion like remark! Perhaps it is because there are so few high saints in the Church that there are so many low sinners outside the Church, since the ungodly can never be powerfully lifted up except by a Church that reaches down from an exalted spiritual plane.

What means that lofty address of the apostle, "Wherefore, holy brethren, *partakers of the heavenly calling*"? (Heb. iii. 1.) The reference is not merely to our final destiny as those who are to be called up to heaven, but to our present service as those who have come down from heaven; sons of God rejoicing in a celestial birth, bringing the air and manners of glory into a world that knows not God. As such we are exhorted to "consider the *Apostle and High Priest* of our profession, Christ Jesus;" an apostle being one who comes forth from God, and an high priest one who goes in unto God. And Christ Jesus not only fulfils both these offices in Himself, as he says, "I came forth from the Father and am come into the world; again I leave the world and go to the Father," but He makes us partakers with Him of the same heavenly calling, sending us into the world, as the Father hath sent Him, and permitting us "to enter into the holiest by the blood of Jesus," as He has entered in by His own blood.

Confessing that our citizenship is in heaven, it should be easily determined what our conduct and bearing towards the world must be. One is expected to pay taxes and make investments where he holds residence. Therefore all calls to bountiful giving and all demands for rigid self-denial are to be esteemed as reasonable assessments, not as gratuities. Christianity is no paradox, in which believers are required to do peculiar things for the sake of being peculiar, and to exhibit startling contradictions for the sake of arousing the contradiction of sinners against themselves. When we are called to lay up treasures in heaven, it is because that is our country; when we are enjoined not to love the world, neither the things that are in the world, it is because this is not our country. Two practical errors spring from an earthly theology, viz., that the world is the Christian's home, and the grave the Christian's hope. On the contrary, one possessed of a clear advent faith would choose for himself such an epitaph as that which Dean Alford composed for his tomb: "*The inn of a traveller on his way to Jerusalem.*" Ah, yes, that is it! A pilgrim's portion, food and raiment and contentment therewith; the mansion which fortune has provided, or the cabin which penury has reared, each alike counted a hospice where one lodges as "a pilgrim and stranger in the earth;" and the grave a narrow inn whose windows look towards the sunrising, where the sojourner sleeps till break of day,—this, without question, is the ideal of the Christian life as outlined in the Gospel.

An impracticable ideal, it will be said. But it was not so in the beginning. To say nothing of apostolic Christianity, let us ask what it was that gave the Christianity of the first two centuries such extraordinary vigor in its conflict with heathenism. An eminent writer, Gerhard Uhlhorn, has shown with a graphic hand that it was just this quality of absolute unworldliness which constituted the secret of its power.[24] The men who conquered the Roman Empire for Christ bore the aspect of invaders from another world, who absolutely refused to be naturalized to this world. Their conduct filled their heathen neighbors with the strangest perplexity: they were so careless of life, so careful of conscience, so prodigal of their own blood, so confident of the overcoming power of the blood of the Lamb, so unsubdued to the customs of the country in which they sojourned, so mindful of the manners of "that country from whence they came out." The help of the world, the patronage of its rulers, the loan of its resources, the use of its methods, they utterly refused, lest by employing these they might compromise their King. An invading army maintained from an invisible base, and placing more confidence in the leadership of an unseen Commander than in all imperial help that might be proffered,—this was what so bewildered and angered the heathen, who often desired to make friends with the Christians without

---

[24] *Conflict of Christianity with Heathenism.*

abandoning their own gods. But there can be no reasonable doubt that that age in which the Church was most completely separated from the world was the age in which Christianity was most victorious in the world.[25]

It was also the era of undimmed hope of the Lord's imminent return from glory, so that it illustrated and enforced both clauses of the great text: "For our citizenship is in heaven, from *whence also we look for the Saviour, the Lord Jesus*"(Phil. iii. 20).

Our Lord set forth His departure from the world under the parable of "a certain nobleman who went into a far country to receive for himself a kingdom, and to return" (Luke xix. 12). As a Roman, living in Judea, on appointment to the governorship of that province, would go to Rome to be invested with office, and then return to rule, so Christ has gone to heaven to be invested with the kingship of the world, and now He and His watchful servants are eagerly waiting for the same thing; He sitting at God's right hand "expecting till His enemies be made His footstool," and they expecting till He shall return to reign over the earth. Of the kingdom, the King and His kinsmen, the same avowal of unearthly origin is made by Christ: "My kingdom is *not of this world*;" "They are *not of the world*, even as I am *not of the world.*" The kingdom is the "kingdom of God," the "kingdom of heaven;" its constituency are those who are "begotten of God," and "born from above." True, this kingdom is now in the world in its rudiments and principles, in its citizens and representatives: those who, like their Lord, have been sent hither to accomplish the work of gathering out a people for His name. But, lest we fall into fatal error, let us not imagine that we are now reigning with Christ on the earth, or that the kingdom of God has been set up in the world. The Church's earthly career during the present age is the exact fac-simile of her Lord's,—a career of exile rather than of exaltation; of rejection rather than of rule; of cross-bearing rather than of scepter-bearing. Grasping at earthly

---

[25] These few sentences from a writer of the second century give a graphic portrait of the Christians of that period: "They inhabit their own country, but as strangers; they bear their part in all things as citizens, and endure all things as aliens. Every foreign country is a fatherland to them, and every fatherland a foreign country. . . . They live in the flesh, but walk not after the flesh. . . . They dwell on earth, but are citizens of heaven. They are poor, and make many rich; they are in want of all things, and they have all things in abundance; they are dishonored, and in dishonor glorified."—*Epistle to Diognetus V.*

sovereignty for the Church while the Sovereign himself is still absent has proved, as we shall show hereafter, the most fruitful root of apostasy. It may be said that this picture of the Church, as despised and rejected in the world, suffering, outcast, and in exile, does not correspond to the facts. Not to the facts of our own generation, we admit, wherein the world is on such excellent terms with Christians. But that it represents the character of the dispensation as a whole cannot be questioned, when we recall the dark ages and martyr ages of the Christian era; the prisons, and racks, and dungeons, and stakes, which stretch on through so large a portion of this age. And the pictures of prophecy are composite pictures, gathering up the main features of the entire dispensation and presenting them in one. Viewed thus, prediction and history perfectly accord.

"The kingdom is now here in mystery, and to be here hereafter in manifestation," one has tersely put it. And to this the predicted destiny of believers corresponds. "*Your life is hid* with Christ in God; when Christ, who is our life, shall appear, then shall ye also *appear with Him in glory*" (Col. iii. 4). "*Sons of God, therefore the world knoweth us not,* because it knew Him not" (1 John iii. 1). "The earnest expectation of the creature waiteth for the *manifestation of the sons of God*" (Rom. viii. 19). "If we suffer, we shall *reign with Him*" (2 Tim. ii. 12). Obscurity, rejection, exile, and trial in the world now; manifestation, vindication, enthronement, when the King comes,—this is the foretold calling of the children of the kingdom. The unprecedented exemption of the Church from persecution, and the extraordinary triumphs of the Gospel which have characterized this nineteenth century, may tend to seduce us into the notion that the kingdom has already come, though the nobleman who had gone into a far country has not yet returned. That we may think truly on this subject, let us hear our Lord's voice, saying: "*Fear not, little flock, for it is your Father's good pleasure to give you the kingdom*" (Luke xii. 32). In spite of widespread conquests of the Gospel the Church is still "a little flock," amid the vast populations of Pagans, Mohammedans, Infidels, and Apostates. This flock in every age has been branded with opprobrium, and torn by persecution, and beaten by hireling shepherds, and the end is not yet; for, as good Samuel Rutherford says, "So long as any portion of Christ's mystical body is out of heaven, Satan will strike at it." However favored in our times, this flock is not the kingdom; but it has the promise of the kingdom, in which rejection shall give place to rule, and crucifixion to coronation. When? "*And when the Chief Shepherd shall appear,* ye shall receive a crown of glory that fadeth not away" (1 Pet. v. 4). Whatever temporary respite from persecution we may enjoy, so that for the time it may be said as of old, "then had the Churches rest," no permanent peace is guaranteed until the Lord's return. "And to you who are troubled, rest with us when the Lord Jesus shall be revealed from heaven" (2 Thess. i. 7).

II.
THE FALL OF THE CHURCH.

WHEN the Church under Constantine became enthroned in the world, she began to be dethroned from her seat "in the heavenly places in Christ Jesus." For then did she forget her high calling, and become enamored of earthly rule and dominion. This, let us not forget, was the fatal temptation through which the Church lost her primitive purity, and brought upon herself all manner of dishonor and apostasy. What a tender prophetic warning of such temptation is contained in that saying of Paul to the Corinthian Christians: "I have espoused you to one husband that I may present you as a chaste virgin to Christ. But I fear lest by any means, as the serpent beguiled Eve through his subtlety, so your minds should be corrupted from the simplicity that is in Christ" (2 Cor. xi. 2). In the world, but not of it, the Church, the Bride of Christ, was to await the return of her Betrothed Husband from heaven, that, arrayed in fine linen, clean and white, which is the righteousness of saints, she might be presented to Him "a glorious Church, not having spot, or wrinkle, or any such thing." If, during the time of her espousal, Satan could only alienate her affections by getting her enamored with the kings of the earth, so that she should accept their dowries instead of her heavenly inheritance, and put on their royal purple instead of her virgin white, his triumph would be assured. And this is literally what he did.

Observe how the temptation was presented first to the Lord Himself by Satan, to seduce Him from His love for the Church, that He should not redeem her with His own blood. "*All the kingdoms of the world and the glory of them*" was the alluring prize which the Tempter set before our Bridegroom. "*All these things will I give Thee if Thou wilt fall down and worship me*" (Matt. iv. 9), was the alluring promise held out to Him. Have we understood the deep reality and significance of this temptation in the wilderness?

Precisely what Satan, "the Prince of this world," proffered—all the kingdoms of the earth—had long ago been pledged to Christ by the Father. But before this inheritance could be realized, He must be despised and rejected of men, crucified and buried, and then raised up to wait an unknown time upon His Father's throne "till His enemies be made His footstool." The Tempter would say, "Why not take the kingdoms of the world *at once*, foregoing the humiliation and the cross and the long rejection by the world?" But the Saviour's resistance of the temptation was prompt and final: "*Get thee behind Me, Satan.*" And when, afterwards, Simon Peter, preoccupied no doubt with the idea of an immediate temporal kingdom for his Lord, repelled Christ's announcement of His approaching crucifixion, saying, "Far be it from Thee, Lord; this shall not be unto thee," Jesus recognized it as the old wilderness temptation reappearing, and met it with the same rebuke: "*Get thee behind Me, Satan*" (Matt. xvi. 23). Thus the Son of God, true to His Father's commission and to His plighted affection for His Bride, whom He must purchase with His own blood, stood firm against this great temptation, accepting a present cross and rejection, instead of a present crown and dominion; choosing to be cast out by a world that knew Him not, until after "the times or seasons which the Father hath put in His own power" should be fulfilled, and the announcement be made, "The kingdoms of this world are become the kingdoms of our Lord and of His Christ, and He shall reign forever and ever."

The second Adam had thus steadfastly resisted the solicitations of the old serpent. Would the second Eve, His Bride, do likewise? For more than two hundred years the Church did remain true to her heavenly citizenship, counting herself a stranger in the earth and looking for her Lord from Heaven. Her uplifted gaze and unworldly attitude were such conspicuous features of the early Church that even unbelieving historians like Gibbon have noted them, and dwelt upon them with a kind of suppressed admiration, that author conceding that, while the hope of Christ's imminent return remained universal, "it was productive of the most salutary effects on the faith and practice of Christians, who lived in the awful expectation of that moment when the globe itself and all the various races of mankind should tremble at the appearance of their divine Judge." The bloody persecutions which reigned from Nero to Diocletian only confirmed this hope,—earthly disenfranchisement making heavenly citizenship more real and dear.

But now the perilous trial of peace was to be encountered. Will the Church endure the test of imperial patronage as she has borne the test of imperial persecution? O Bride of Immanuel, made "dead to the law by the body of Christ *that ye should be married to another, even to Him who was raised from the dead*" (Rom. vii. 4), alas for the day when thou didst receive the kings of the earth for thy lovers, and, forgetful of thy Lord's promise, "I appoint unto you a kingdom as My Father hath appointed unto Me," didst accept a throne from the princes of this world! Earth's sovereignty had long since been pledged to the Church as well as to Christ: "And the kingdom and dominion and the greatness of the kingdom under the whole heaven shall be given to the people of the saints of the Most High" (Dan. vii. 27). But the time for its acquisition was definitely fixed at the coming of the Son of man in the clouds of heaven. For the Church to accept it in the present age was to fall before the very temptation where her Lord had stood firm.

If we look upon that famous assembly, the Council of Nicea, A. D. 325, what a clear dividing line does it present between the old and the new, between the Church heavenly that had been, and the Church earthly that was to be! Here on the one hand were the true successors of the apostles, bearing in their bodies the marks of the Lord Jesus; their maimed limbs, and sightless eyes, and marred visages telling most expressively how, up to this time, the servants of Jesus had been "filling up that which is behind of the afflictions of Christ in the flesh for His body's sake, which is the Church."

But here, on the other hand, in strange contrast with these, was that central figure, arrayed in rich robes and seated on a golden chair in the midst of the assembly,—Constantine, the head of the Church. "What gain to our cause," whispered ambitious bishops, "that now we have a Christian emperor who will throw over us the shield of his protection and defend the orthodox faith with the sword!" "Alas, what loss!" might have sighed the angels, as they witnessed the nuptials of the Bride of Christ with the kings of the earth. But did not Constantine have a supernatural seal set upon his imperial patronage of the Church in that vision of the flaming cross displayed in the heavens with its motto, IN THIS SIGN CONQUER? Considering the real character of the emperor, as afterwards unfolded, a faith which should credit the alleged vision as from God would be far more difficult than a credulity which should ascribe it to the arch-tempter. For what was that cross by which the Church was henceforth to seek her conquests? An eminent historian has described the startling impression made upon his mind by the sight of a crucifix which was shown him in Italy,—a crucifix exquisitely carved, and studded with the rarest jewels, but which at the touch of a secret spring flew open, and proved itself to be a case for holding a keen-edged and glittering Roman dagger.

There is a cross in which an apostle was wont to glory as that whereby the world was crucified unto him, and he unto the world; there is a cross concerning which our Lord spake, saying: "If any man will come after Me, let him deny himself and take up his cross and follow Me." But how utterly remote from these that cross which began to sway the Church from the age of Constantine,—that cross which carried the dagger of persecution in the crucifix of superstition, thus supplanting "the sword of the Spirit" by "the sword of the magistrate," in order to further the gospel of peace!

This fall from heavenly to earthly citizenship was accompanied, moreover, by a gradual exchange of spiritual worship for carnal superstitions. Worse than carnal, indeed! Satan, who had tempted the Church into accepting earthly dominion from his hands, now seduced her into mixing his own ritual with her simple, primitive services. For we must not forget that, according to the explicit teaching of Scripture, paganism is really demonism. "The things which the Gentiles sacrifice, *they sacrifice to demons, and not to God*" (1 Cor. x. 20), says the apostle. Whether the deluded votaries of Jupiter and Mars knew it or not, it was really true that demons were the instigators and recipients of their worship. Idolatry is always and everywhere the religion of Satan, ordained for stealing from God the homage of human hearts and turning it to himself. And so, little by little, the elements of paganism began to mingle with the worship of Christ,—holy water, candles, the wafer, images, processions, the adoration of saints and relics, the idolatry of the cross, and much more,—of all which we may assert confidently what Cardinal Newman concedes concerning the first, that they were originally "*the very instruments and appendages of demon-worship.*"[26]

But though the Church has thus been corrupted, out of it a faithful number has been preserved to constitute the hidden Bride of Christ. Observe how graphically this is shown in the sealing of the one hundred and forty-four thousand in the seventh chapter of Revelation,—a passage not hard to

---

[26] *Development*, pp 359, 360.

understand if we bear in mind, as always in studying the Apocalypse, that Scripture explains Scripture, and that history repeats history.

In the eighth chapter of Ezekiel we find God denouncing the heathen abominations which have been mixed with the worship of His sanctuary,—"the image of jealousy," the "weeping for Tammuz," and the eastward posture in which men "worshipped the sun towards the East." On account of these pollutions the Lord commands fearful judgments upon His people. But, before these judgments commence, He bids His messengers: "Go through the midst of the city, through the midst of Jerusalem, and *set a mark upon the foreheads of the men that sigh and cry for all the abominations that be done in the midst thereof.*" As the destroyers go forth the injunction is: "*But come not near any man upon whom is the mark.*" Here is a sealed and spared remnant in the midst of the prevailing Jewish apostasy. Turn now to the corresponding story in the Apocalypse (Rev. vii.). The prophetic drama opens with the Church in her primitive exaltation, seated with Christ in heavenly places; then the seals are unloosed, unfolding the successive chapters of Christian history,—conquest, conflict, famine, and pestilence; the "Come!" "Come!" "Come!" "Come!" is heard breaking in before each opening era, answering in majestic antiphon the Lord's "Behold, I come quickly," and showing the Church still true to her ancient hope; the martyrs, "slain for the word of God and the testimony which they held," invoke their Redeemer, "How long, O Lord?" Then comes the crash of falling paganism, with the affrighted cry of the heathen before "the wrath of the Lamb," and Christianity, that was so long upon the scaffold and at the stake, is now upon the throne of the Cæsars.

But, alas, as we have seen, the Church, that has been "more than conqueror" through defeat, is now more than vanquished through victory! For, having overthrown paganism, she became herself gradually paganized, and her worship corrupted with mixtures of heathen religion which the Scriptures call the worship of demons,—the employment of images and pictures, which of old provoked the Lord to jealousy; the turning towards the east, after the manner of the Babylonish sun-worshippers; the signing with the cross,[27] which was long connected with the sensual worship of Tammuz. In fine, the identical abominations which God had denounced in the Jewish sanctuary were now found in the Christian Church. And once more avenging scourges are let loose on Christendom—Saracen and Turkish invasions—to punish its inhabitants, "*that they should not worship demons, and idols of gold, and silver, and brass, and stone, and of wood*" (Rev. ix. 20).

But before judgment begins, God's sealing and separation again take place: "And I saw another angel ascending from the east, *having the seal of the living God*, saying, Hurt not the earth, neither the sea nor the trees, *till we have sealed the servants of God in their foreheads.*"[28] The sealed company whose description follows is an elect company out of the tribes of spiritual Israel; a small company compared with the great mass of nominal Christians; a perfect company, "*one hundred and forty-four thousand.*" It is the foursquare multitude, identical with the four-square city, which appears in the twentieth chapter, coming down from God out of Heaven, and which is explained to be "*the Bride, the Lamb's wife.*" It is a company "sealed with the Holy Spirit of promise," in contrast with the vast throngs of unconverted heathen who have been sealed with the sign of the cross; and as chosen and faithful, it exhibits the twofold signature of the seal of God,—"*The Lord knoweth them that are His,*" and "*Let every one that nameth the name of Christ depart from iniquity*" (2 Tim. ii. 19). This true and unseduced Bride of Christ we meet throughout the Apocalypse, as we do throughout the whole course of Christian history. Whether as Waldensian, or Huguenot, or Lollard, she is ever hated by the apostate Church. But she preserves her virginity unstained, keeps herself undefiled from the harlot Church and her daughters, and when all Christendom has become earthly she maintains her heavenly citizenship;

---

[27] Julian, the emperor (361 A. D.), taunts the Christians with their idolatry, saying, "Ye worship the wood of the cross, making shadowy figures of it in the forehead, and painting it at the entrance of your houses."—See Note B.

[28] Rev. vii. 2, 3. In the Apocalypse, where Jewish people, Jewish temple, and Jewish rites stand for corresponding Christian facts, we have no doubt that this sealed company represents spiritual Israel,—real Christians out of the great multitude of nominal Christians. Dean Alford's challenge, to those who hold that *literal Israel* is here meant, is decisive. He asks whether "the Holy Jerusalem, descending out of heaven from God" (Rev. xxi. 10), must be taken to be the residence of literal Jews, because it bears the names of "the twelve tribes of the children of Israel." Few would admit this inference, we believe.

now hidden out of sight, and now seen standing with the Lamb upon Mount Zion. So that to the end, as in the beginning, we greet her with the divine salutation, "But ye are come unto Mount Zion, and unto the city of the living God, the heavenly Jerusalem."

We shall meet her again in her final presentation to the Bridegroom; but for the present we must further trace the fortunes of her fallen sister.

III.
THE ADVENT OF ANTICHRIST.

OUT of the apostasy comes the Antichrist. To look for him without the Church in latter-day Judaism, or against the Church in latter-day infidelity, is equally to miss the clear marks of identification which have been set for our warning in "the sure word of prophecy."

Exhorting the Thessalonian Christians "by the coming of our Lord Jesus Christ and by our gathering together unto Him," the Apostle admonishes them not to be deceived: "*For it will not be, except the falling away come first, and the man of sin be revealed, the son of perdition, he that opposeth and exalteth himself against all that is called God or that is worshipped; so that he sitteth in the temple of God, setting himself forth as God*" (2 Thess. ii. 3, R. V.). Here is the great Pauline prediction of Antichrist; and how rigidly does its language bind us to the conception of a dreadful enemy of God, springing up within the Christian Church! "*Except the apostasy come first*," the words read exactly. It can be "no political or politico-religious falling away" that is here indicated, as Ellicott truly says; but, according to the scriptural use of the term, "that religious and spiritual apostasy, that falling away from faith in Christ, of which the revelation of Antichrist shall be the concluding and most appalling phenomenon." And looking backward over the history of the Church for eighteen hundred years, we ask how the prediction could be more literally fulfilled than in the astonishing eclipse of pagan and idolatrous superstition under whose shadow two thirds of nominal Christendom now rests. So we may premise that we shall find the answer to this mysterious prophecy in the line of popes having their seat of authority in Rome, and extending their rule through more than twelve centuries of the Christian era.

In examining this prediction we begin with that expression which is most central and suggestive: "*He sitteth in the temple of God, setting himself forth as God*." The interpretation which applies these words to the material temple rebuilt in Jerusalem is lacking both in accuracy and significance,—in accuracy, since there is no undisputed instance in the New Testament where the phrase, ὁ ναός τοῦ θεοῦ, the temple of God, is applied to the Jewish temple; and in significance, since it would be a matter of indifferent interest to Gentile

Christians that some distant pretender was to arise who should win the acceptance and homage of the Jews.[29] Scripture interprets Scripture; and when we hear false witnesses accusing Christ of saying, "I am able to destroy the temple of God and to build it in three days," we have only to turn to another text to find that in what he said, "*He spake of the temple of His body*" (John ii. 21). So when a Judaizing interpretation would lead us, from this phrase of the Apostle, to imagine a future temple rebuilt in Jerusalem, enthroning an infidel Antichrist, we have only to collate the passages in which the expression occurs to find how invariably it stands for Christ's mystical body, the Church, considered as a whole or in its members: "*Know ye not that ye are the temple of God, and that the Spirit of God dwelleth in you?*" (1 Cor. iii. 16.)

Here is wisdom; for why is the Church called the temple of God? Because indwelt by the Spirit, presided in by the Holy Ghost. When this temple—the redeemed Church of Christ—was dedicated on the day of Pentecost, the Spirit descended in the semblance of tongues of fire, and it "*sat—ἐκάθισεν—upon each one of them.*" Henceforth the body of believers, sanctified and sealed, is the true *Cathedra*, where the Spirit sits; the real "Holy See," or seat of the Holy One. Sanctity or sacrilege, therefore, is indicated by this word "sit," according as it is applied to God presiding in His own house, or to man thrusting himself into God's place. Observe how reverently the apostle Peter recognizes the Spirit's presence and primacy in the Church so soon as He is come. Rebuking the sin of Ananias, he says: "Why hath Satan filled thy heart *to lie to the Holy Ghost?*" "Thou hast not lied unto men, *but unto God*" (Acts v.

---

[29] For the significance of this phrase, ὁ ναός τοῦ θεοῦ, see the following texts, the only ones where it occurs: 1 Cor. iii. 16; 1 Cor. iii. 17; 1 Cor. iii. 17; 11 Cor. vi. 16; II Cor. vi. 16; Rev. iii. 12; Rev. xi. 1-19. Of the word ναός alone, we beg it to be noticed that after the institution of the Christian Church it is never once applied to the temple in Jerusalem. Twenty-five times in the Acts the Jewish temple is spoken of, but the word ἱερόν is used in every instance, never ναός. Neither is the latter word once employed in any epistle to designate the Hebrew temple. How could God call that His temple (ναός) when He had ceased to dwell therein (νάω),— "*Behold, your house is left unto you, desolate*"? How surely must the word apply to the Christian Church after that God by the Holy Ghost had taken up His abode in it!—"*An holy temple (ναός) in the Lord, in whom ye also are builded together for an habitation of God through the Spirit.*" We believe that a candid exegesis of this phrase ὁ ναός τοῦ θεοῦ —fixes the seat of the man of sin within the sphere of the Christian Church, as certainly as the designation of the seven hills fixes the seat of the woman of sin in the city of Rome.

3). No thought of His own primacy here! Mark with wonder, also, the holy deference which the ascended Lord Himself yields to the Spirit, now that, as the promised Paraclete, He has taken His place in the Church. Seven times in his post-ascension gospel—the epistles to the seven churches—we hear Him say: "He that hath an ear, *let him hear what the Spirit saith unto the churches;*" as though to teach us that, while the Spirit is in office as President and Teacher, even the glorified Christ will not intrude into His seat; but will commend us to His guidance, even as while He was on earth the Father commended His disciples to Him, saying, "This is My beloved Son, *hear ye Him.*"

We are prepared thus to comprehend the presumption and blasphemy which it would imply for a man to sit in the Spirit's seat in the Temple of God. And we know that one of the most conspicuous traits of the early apostasy was clerisy, the thrusting of man into the place of rule and authority which belong to the Spirit; that this tendency constantly strengthened till the bishops, instead of humbly heeding the apostolic injunction to feed the flock over which the Holy Ghost had made them overseers, began to lord it over that flock, rearing a primacy out of the pastorate, and a papacy out of the primacy, till the evil culminated in the sovereign pontiff usurping the place of the Holy Ghost. For since the Holy Ghost is Christ's true and only Vicar on earth,—"*another Paraclete*" sent to take the place of the ascended Lord,—what is he who should claim to be the Vicar of Christ but a usurper of the Spirit's seat in the temple of God?

All the dark outlines of Paul's prophetic picture of the Antichrist harmonize with this interpretation. He is called "*The man of sin,*" as though to mark his utter contrast to the true pastor, whom the Scriptures name "*The man of God.*" But could the long succession of popes be designated by this individual name, "*The man?*" Yes; the elect Church, extending through all ages, is called in Scripture "*one new man*" (Eph. ii. 15). The true line of spiritual ministers is evidently intended by "*the man of God* thoroughly furnished," named in the Epistle to Timothy. So with other terms in which the singular is used for the plural: the succession of the Jewish priesthood is certainly meant in the statement in the Epistle to the Hebrews, "Into the second went *the high priest* alone once every year." Indeed, if it be urged that the name Antichrist—ὁ ἀντίχριστος—must mean an individual man, we find that this is not necessary, since the whole body of believers throughout the dispensation is called by its counterpart "The Christ," ὁ Χριστός (1 Cor. xii. 12). Thus Scripture, as well as the common usage, in which we speak of the royal or of the ecclesiastical succession as "the king," or "the bishop," justify us in interpreting "the man of sin" to mean the line of pontiffs. As to the character indicated by the words, must we not admit its fulfilment to the uttermost in the pontificate? Whatever virtue or mildness may have appeared in single instances, we are to remember that the pictures of prophecy are composite photographs, giving the main features combined as revealed throughout the age. Who can deny that many of the popes have been monsters of iniquity, or that the great majority have stained their hands with the blood of saints? If so, does not this language sufficiently express their blended likeness?

Yet deeper and more dreadful grow the shadows with which inspiration paints the portrait: "The man of sin, *the son of perdition.*" Only one has borne this latter name, Judas Iscariot, who with a kiss betrayed his Lord, and, with a "Hail, Master!" on his lips, delivered Him to His enemies. And who was Judas, that his significant name should be thrown forward upon the coming Antichrist? He was an apostate bishop,—"*His bishopric let another take*" (Acts i. 20). He was a thief who had the bag, and who, in order to enrich himself, sold his Lord for thirty pieces of silver. Oh appalling counter-reality which we see emerging from the shadows of history! the pontifical bag-bearer, rich with untold treasures purloined from his poor flock, delivering up the Body of Christ evermore to death, as the first betrayer did the Head, till the enthroned Redeemer must have groaned again and again, as of old: "Why persecutest thou Me?" Revolting as it is to our Christian charity to dwell upon these things, we are compelled, in a time when a speculative interpretation is joining hands with a sacramental apostasy, to veil the face of Antichrist. Yet, if only once in the ages,—after Waldensian slaughter or St. Bartholomew's massacre,—we could see this vicar of Iscariot flinging down his silver and crying, "I have betrayed the innocent blood," what haste would we make to throw the mantle of forgetfulness over his ghastly deeds!

The marks of correspondence between this counter-Christ and the true are most striking at every point. He has his *Parousia* and his *Apocalypse*—his coming and his revelation—as does the Christ. The Son of God enters His earthly career through incarnation,—"Great is *the mystery of godliness*, He who was manifested in the flesh,"—and the son of perdition does the same: "*The mystery of iniquity* doth already work." As it was said of the Lord's betrayer, "Then entered Satan into Judas Iscariot," so the beginning of this enemy is through a dark, mysterious entering in of the Evil One for corrupting the Church. The mystery of godliness is God humbling Himself to become man; the mystery of iniquity is man exalting himself to become God,—"Ye shall be as gods." The mystery of godliness is loyalty; the Son of God, through the Holy Spirit, rendering perfect obedience to the will and word of the Father: the mystery of iniquity is lawlessness, ἀνομία; the son of perdition, through "the spirit that now worketh in the children of disobedience," subverting God's law, and rule, and order in the Church. In the one we see Christ emptying Himself of His glory; in the other we see Antichrist filling himself with his glory, so that he "opposeth and exalteth himself above every one called God or an object of worship," and "sitteth in the temple of God, setting himself forth as God."[30] How marvellously has this latter prediction been realized! "*Domine Deus!*" If but once we heard these words addressed to the pope by his allowance, it should lead us, as the students of this prophecy, to ask, "Art thou he that should come?" What if employed repeatedly, and with every variety of adoration? Alexander VI., the Nero of the Pontificate, as he has been called, moving to his consecration, passes under a triumphal arch, on which is inscribed: "Cæsar was a man; *Alexander is a God.*" Marcellus, in an address to Pope Leo X. at the fifth Lateran Council, exclaims, "Thou art another God on earth"—*tu denique alter Deus in terris*. Gregory II. boasts to the Greek emperor: "All the kings of the West reverence the pope as a God on earth." Pope Nicholas writes: "Wherefore if those things which I do be said to be done, not of man, but of God, *what can you, make me but God?* Again, if the prelates of the Church be called and counted of Constantine for gods, I,

---

[30] "'*As God, showing Himself that He is God.*' For many hundred years, to this day, the Roman pontiffs have literally fulfilled this prophecy of St. Paul. When Cornelius, the centurion, fell down at Peter's feet and worshipped him, St. Peter forbade him, saying, '*Stand up! I myself also am a man.*' But the self-called successors of St. Peter *sit in the temple of God as God.* For many centuries each of them, at his inauguration, has taken his seat in God's Church, upon God's altar, and, so sitting, has been adored by men falling down before him and kissing his feet."—Bishop Wordsworth on the Apocalypse, p. 394.

then, being above all prelates, seem by this reason to be *above all gods.*" These instances of deification, if there were no more, would fill out every line and specification of this Pauline prediction; while that culminating act of 1870—the placing of the crown of infallibility upon the head of the pope by the Ecumenical Council—would set the attesting seal of literal history to this astonishing word of literal prophecy.

We know how some, at this point, have started on an adventurous hunt into the future for an Antichrist who is at once a God-denier and a God-pretender; since the apostle John has declared concerning this terrible personage that he "denieth the Father and the Son." But the candid reader has only to compare this word "deny" as employed by John with its use by Paul, and Peter, and Jude, in their predictions of the falling away, to see that the reference is beyond question to the denial of apostasy, and not to the denial of infidelity; to such as "profess that they know God, but in works deny Him," and not to such as are avowedly and openly atheistic.[31] The anomaly of bald infidel worship, exacted by one who at once deifies and undeifies, has no place, we are persuaded, in this prophecy. Nor has that other conception of a Napoleonic demigod drunk with the infatuation of world-rule,—a conception which has greatly colored the imaginations of many expositors. That the man of sin is identical with the "little horn" of Daniel, and the "beast" of the Apocalypse, is clear enough; and that as such he is a temporal ruler, no one doubts. And so has he proved; for when has the world seen a line of world-sovereigns like the popes? But can we imagine such a blending, in any single infidel man, of secular and spiritual imperialism as is foreshadowed in this compound prediction of Scripture, and as is fulfilled in this double-headed ruler in the Vatican? The pontiffs are the lineal successors of the Cæsars, as they claim to be of the apostles. Mr. Pember, in describing this combination of office, gives a perfect description of the sovereign pontiff, though he did not intend it as such:—

---

[31] See Titus i. 16, 2 Peter ii. 1, Jude 4. The latest dictionary of the Greek New Testament—the Grimm, edited by Thayer—gives this as the second definition of ἀρνέομαι, to deny: "'Αρνέομαι. God and Christ, is used of those who, by cherishing and disseminating pernicious opinions and immorality, *are adjudged to have apostatized from God and Christ.*" 1 John ii. 22 (cf. iv. 2; 2 John vii. 11); Jude 4; 2 Pet. ii. 1.

"At length, however, Julius Cæsar, who had previously accepted the office of Pontifex Maximus, solved the difficulty by constituting himself emperor. He thus became the first Roman in whom the powers of the Pontifex and the Imperator were combined, and was probably the first to be recognized as the head of the Oriental priesthood,—the Roman pontificate having previously been distinct from and inferior to the Chaldean, with which it was thenceforth identified. He was consequently declared to be divine, and exercised a wonderful influence over his army and the people, even going to the length of openly *prescribing to the latter for whom they should vote.* And lastly he corrected the calendar and *changed times* by inserting two additional months, in accordance with the pontifical prerogative, which gave him his title of King of the Ages. The power which he had acquired descended to his successors; so that in the statues of the emperors, the ring is always engraved with the figure of a *lituus,* or crosier, to indicate the highest quality of imperatorial rank,—that of Pontifex Maximus."[32] And the popes are the successors of these successors.

Such is the figure which history presents as its answer to prophecy. Is it only the eye of bigotry that can detect a likeness between the two?

The germs of this evil system were growing in the apostle's day,—"*The mystery of iniquity doth already work.*" Is it credible that it should have continued operating through eighteen centuries, in order to bring forth some yet future short-lived, infidel Antichrist, so transcendently wicked that all which has gone before, with its unspeakable record of blood and blasphemy, is only an indifferent prototype of him? If charity could bias our interpretation at all, which it must not, how little mercy have they who, in order to relieve the papacy of this stigma, darken our future with such an appalling apparition! Moreover, such a conception puts a strain upon our credulity greater than it can bear. For when we study Satan's career in Scripture and in history, we find that open infidelity is little in his line. His way has ever been to masquerade in the symbols and sacraments of the Church; to manipulate the machinery of spurious miracles; to put on a sad countenance as the hypocrites do, that behind it he may mock at God. Therefore the epiphany of "that Wicked One" should be looked for in a

---

[32] Antichrist, Babylon, and the Coming Kingdom, p. 81.

feigned religiousness rather than in a blatant atheism; as it is tersely said in the *Noble Lesson* of the Waldensians: "Antichrist is the falsehood of eternal damnation covered with the appearance of truth and righteousness of Christ and his Spouse."[33]

For this reason we are not surprised at the prediction of startling wonder-working as signalizing the advent of this pseudo-Christ, "*whose coming is after the working of Satan in all power, and signs, and wonders of falsehood.*" One who is at all acquainted with the history of the Middle Ages need not be told how exactly the papal reality fits this prediction; how the chaste and artless miracles of the primitive Church were travestied by those of the mediæval Church in the grotesque signs and wonders alleged to have been wrought at saints' tombs, and through the agency of martyrs' bones and sacred relics. Thus was the man of sin to authenticate his ministry "*in all deceit of unrighteousness for them that are perishing;*" and the issue would be that God should "*send them a working of delusion that they should believe the lie, that they may all of them be judged who believed not the truth.*"[34] And so has it come to pass; the assumptions of the priesthood culminating in a deified man, and the working of delusion culminating in a deified wafer. A devout minister in the Church of England, crying out in pain at the apostasy now repeating itself in his own communion, boldly says, concerning the miracle of transubstantiation: "The crowning error into which the visible Church was by degrees led—the process of Satanic inspiration extending from the eighth to the thirteenth century—was, that the priesthood possessed a divine power to locate the Lord Jesus Christ on an earthly altar, and to lift him up, under the veils of bread and wine, to the adoration of the people. It is in this blasphemous fraud that the apostle Paul's prophecy finds its accurate fulfilment. Of the apostasy forerunning the second coming of Christ he says, that the deluded followers of the Lawless One should believe 'THE LIE,'— τό ψεῦδος. Of all the impostures that the Father of Lies ever palmed upon a credulous world, this doctrine, which both logically and theologically repeats millions of times the humiliation of the Blessed Redeemer, necessarily

---

[33] "*Antichrist es falseta de damnation œterna cuberta de specie de la verita e de la justitia de Christ e de la soa sposa.*"—*Des Eglises Vaudoises*, chap. xiv.

[34] Thess. ii. 9, 10 (Ellicott's translation).

transcends all! Hence it is that the definite article is placed by the Holy Ghost before this word 'lie.'"[35]

Of "the mouth speaking great things and blasphemies," ascribed to this being both in Daniel and Revelation, we have only to inquire what mouth-assumption could surpass that contained in the well-known Bull Unam Sanctam of Boniface VIII.: "*It is essential for salvation for every human creature to be subject to the Roman pontiff.*" Blasphemy means usurpation of the prerogatives of the Deity rather than profane denial. When the Jews accused Jesus of this sin, this was the ground: "Why does this man speak blasphemies?" *Who can forgive sins but God alone?* Again: "For a good work we stone Thee not; but for blasphemy, and because *Thou, being a man, makest Thyself God.*" Does not the man of Rome stand openly convicted on both these grounds?

In the expression, "*He who now letteth,*" we have one of the most significant touches in the whole picture. What hindered the manifestation of Antichrist? "And now *ye know* what withholdeth," says the apostle. If they did know, and passed the secret from lip to lip, tradition on this point is valuable. Hence when we find that it was the well-nigh unanimous understanding among the Christian fathers, from those who touched hands with the apostles onward, that it was the Roman Empire that must be taken out of the way before the man of sin could be revealed, we have strong reason to credit this opinion. And mark how the reserve of the apostle, in not mentioning this hindering power, bears out this interpretation. If, as some now say, it was the Holy Spirit that was intended, we can see no reason why He should not have been distinctly named; but if it was the Roman Empire, there is every ground for the apostle's withholding the fact from his epistle, and committing it only to oral tradition. For the epistle would be publicly read in the churches, and its contents reported, perhaps, to the ears of the rulers. To say that the empire, which was held to be eternal, was about to pass away, would savor of treason, and would form a just ground for persecution. And therefore, it would seem, the apostle gave it out as a whispered secret: "*Remember ye not that when I was yet with you I told you these things? And now ye know what withholdeth that he might be revealed in his time*" (2 Thes.

---

[35] Ormiston, *Satan of Scripture*, p. 126.

ii. 6). For once tradition has authority, since in this chapter the apostle not only enjoins that those addressed "obey our word by this epistle," but also "hold to the *traditions* which ye have been taught, *whether by word or our epistle.*" And we know on the fullest testimony that the opinion named was held as a tradition apostolical in the early Church; and as such it has come down to us. If, then, the Thessalonians knew, and that which they knew has been, with reasonable certainty, reported to us, is it presumptuous that we should strongly believe?

If we are right at this point, a strong light is thrown upon the question raised in the early part of the chapter, whether a singular noun can stand for a succession of individuals. This hindering power is *"he that letteth,"* which antiquity interpreted to mean the succession of emperors. On which Bishop Wordsworth remarks, "*As he that letteth* is a public person or series of persons, so is he *that sitteth* also;" the one being the succession of emperors, and the other being the succession of popes.

And here comes in the most weighty consideration that so it was, that the papacy did actually emerge upon the subsidence of the empire. Cardinal Manning, who certainly has no prepossession in favor of the view we are advocating, writes thus: "*The possession of the pontiffs commences with the abandonment of Rome by the emperors. . . . No sovereign has ever reigned in Rome since, except the Vicar of Jesus Christ.*"[36] Singular coincidence! does the reader exclaim? No, not singular; it was bound to be so, on account of certain words which an apostle wrote centuries before under the inspiration of the Holy Ghost. Prophecy is the mould in which history is cast; and no violence of man, no convulsions of nations, can either break that mould or constrain the course of history, that the one should not answer to the other point by point, feature by feature. It is for the Christian interpreter to note such correspondences as they occur, counting each conformation as a confirmation for establishing the sure word of prophecy. A system of exposition which withdraws our attention from these coincidences, and sets

---

[36] "By a singular arrangement of Divine Providence, as we have said on a former occasion, it happened that the Roman Empire, having fallen, and being divided into many kingdoms and divers states, the Roman pontiff, in the midst of such great variety of kingdoms, and in the actual state of human society, was invested with his civil authority."—*The Pope's Allocution*, 1866.

us to gazing into blank space for something to emerge, of which not even the shadow is in sight, we cannot think profitable. There are things to come which ought powerfully to attract our attention, but our eyes should not be so holden thereby that we cannot see what is passing and what has already come to pass upon the earth. Such correspondences of history with prophecy, of fact with prediction, as these that we have pointed out, cannot occur by chance. And in view of them we may as certainly hold the papacy to be the fulfilment of Paul's prediction of the Antichrist as we hold the face of a coin to be the fulfilment of the die in which it was struck.[37]

We end where we began,—with the temple of God. The dreadful prediction of the destiny of the man of sin is in the words: "Whom the Lord shall consume with the spirit of His mouth, and shall destroy with the brightness of His coming." Behold how the consuming has been going on within the last few centuries, especially during our own time; so that an eminent writer has declared that in the downfall of the temporal power the papacy met with the heaviest loss which has befallen her in a thousand years. But of the rest how can we speak but with an unutterable awe and pity: "*Whom He shall destroy with the brightness of His appearing.*" For what? "Know ye not that ye are the temple of God, and that the Spirit of God dwelleth in you? *If any man defile the temple of God, him will God destroy. For the temple of God is holy, which temple are ye*" (1 Cor. iii. 17). What language can tell how this temple has been defiled? The heathen rites and ceremonies corrupting the worship of Christ; the idols and the sacrilege; the worship of the queen of heaven; the blood of God's saints staining His own courts; the blasphemy of a man professing to forgive sin; of a man snatching

---

[37] It is coming to be admitted even by futurist interpreters that the word "Antichrist" signifies a vice-Christ, rather than an open opponent of Christ. Andrew Jukes says: "I am satisfied that, according to the derivation of the word, Antichrist means primarily '*in the place of Christ,*' rather than '*against Christ.*' Ἀντί—in Latin, *vice*, whence we get the word *Vicar*, the very title claimed in reference to Christ by the Pope of Rome—is literally '*in the place of.*'" He cites, among others, the following examples: Ἀνθύπατος (Acts xiii. 7), the deputy, or proconsul, not "against the consul," but "in the place of the consul;" Ἀντεπίσκοπος (Gregor. Naz.), a vice-bishop, one acting for the bishop. That this is not a merely modern and Protestant interpretation will appear from the fact that Lactantius (260-330) speaks thus of this personage: "Now this is he who is called Antichrist; but *he shall falsely call himself Christ,* and shall fight against the truth."— *The Divine Institutes*, lib. vii., cap. xix.

the attribute of Divine infallibility; of a man receiving worship from his fellows; in fine, of a man sitting in the seat of the Holy Ghost, shutting the mouth of God's Spirit,—the Holy Scriptures,—and bidding the Church hear only his own "mouth speaking great things." Idolatry of Mary; idolatry of the mass; idolatry of the cross! How solemnly sounds God's word in view of it all! "*And what agreement hath a temple of God with idols?*" (2 Cor. vi. 16, R. V.) Do we not know, if we have read the Scriptures, that it is such desecration of His house, and such defiling of His worship, which have ever called down the severest judgments of God? Let us recall the fact, not that we may redouble our denunciation of an apostate Church, but that we may search our own sanctuaries, with a lighted candle, to see if aught of the corrupting leaven be found among us.

What our eyes see is, again, an astonishing seal set to the truth of this great prediction. Who has not heard the oft-quoted saying that the condition of the Jews in the present dispensation is the most striking verification of the truth of the Scripture? Just as was predicted, they have been scattered, peeled, and subjected to daily death; and yet here they are preserved as a distinct people, a burning bush ever aflame with persecuting fires, but not consumed.

So has the line of pontiffs continued.[38] Taking its rise in the beginnings of the age, gradually strengthening and maturing till fully developed, with temporal and spiritual sovereignty centring in one head, it has lived on for more than twelve hundred years, and there it sits to-day on its seat in Rome, in spite of every likelihood that it would long ago have passed away, the longest line of rulers the Western world has ever seen. As the Jewish succession remains unbroken, that the last generation of cast-off Israel may confront the descending Lord at His advent, looking on Him whom they pierced, and

---

[38] "*And power was given unto him to continue forty and two months*" (Rev. xiii. 5). This period of Antichrist's duration we hold to be, according to the "year-day theory," twelve hundred and sixty years. To those who deride such interpretation as strained, and insist that the words mean three years and a half, we reply: What expositor has interpreted the *ten days' tribulation* in Rev. ii. 10 to be ten literal days? But if the Holy Spirit meant years, in the Apocalypse, why did He not say years? it is replied. Why, when He meant churches and ministers, and kingdoms and kings and epochs, did He say candle-sticks, and stars, and beasts, and horns, and trumpets? Yet, having used these miniature symbols of greater things, how fitting that the accompanying time should also be in miniature! To use literal dates would distort the imagery, as though you should put a life-sized eye in a small-sized photograph.

mourning because of Him with saving penitence that "so all Israel shall be saved;" so likewise the long succession of hierarchs continues, that the last Pontifex Maximus may stand face to face with the Lord at His appearing, and receive his doom, in the cutting off of his usurping line forever. As we read all this, let it be with bowed heads and with weeping eyes, while we ponder the lesson, once more, of the terrible consequences of pride, and ambition, and worldliness, when permitted to run their course in the Church of God.

IV.
THE BRIDE OF ANTICHRIST.

AMONG the presumptuous titles ascribed to the Papal Antichrist is that of "True Lord and Husband of the Church." If he is such, we must find in Scripture the portraiture of his bride, that we may carefully distinguish her from the wife of the Lamb. As the most complete and graphic picture of the "man of sin" is found in the second chapter of Thessalonians, so the most vivid portrayal of the woman of sin with whom he is allied is found in the seventeenth chapter of Revelation. Here we behold her introduced under the name of "*The great harlot that sitteth upon many waters*" and she is pictured as riding upon a beast with "*seven heads and ten horns.*" These symbols are interpreted for us by the Spirit of God, so that in our study of this mystery we have a divinely revealed clue with which to begin. "*The waters which thou sawest where the harlot sitteth are peoples, and multitudes, and nations, and tongues.*" Wide dominion and far-reaching sway over the inhabitants of earth are here indicated. "*The seven heads are the seven mountains on which the woman sitteth.*" In poetry and in history, on monuments and on coins, Rome is known as "the seven-hilled city." Propertius thus speaks of her:—

> The city high on seven hills
> That rules the boundless earth."

The designation is so exact that there is a well-nigh unanimous consent among Romanist and Protestant interpreters alike, that the ancient imperial city on the Tiber is hereby pointed out, though the former contend that the prophecy relates to pagan Rome. "The great harlot" is a term equally clear in its significance; it being the representation of a fallen and apostatized Church. "*How is the faithful city become an harlot!*" (Isa. i. 21) exclaims Jehovah in His lament over backsliding Jerusalem. "*Thou hast played the harlot with many lovers*" (Jer. iii. 1) he cries again. And once more: "*Though Israel play the harlot, let not Judah offend*" (Hos. iv. 15). Thus in the Scripture's own light we discern this mistress to be the faithless Church who, having violated her betrothment, and having ceased to look for the return of her affianced Husband, has admitted others into his place and become the paramour of the kings of the earth. Most distinctly, then, are the character, and dominion, and residence of this ecclesiastical woman defined.

If we turn now to the prophetic description of the woman's dress, we are almost startled by its realistic character: "*And the woman was arrayed in purple and scarlet color, and decked with gold and precious stones and pearls.*" Who does not know that scarlet and purple are as truly "the colors" of the papacy as the red, white and blue are of the United States? In the *Ceremoniale Romanum*—an ancient book of directions,—the dress and adornments with which the pope must be clad on assuming his office are minutely described. Of the different articles of attire specified, five are *scarlet*. A vest covered with *pearls*, and a mitre adorned with *gold and precious stones* are also named in the prescribed apparel. Nor need we go back to so early authority on this point. Our own eyes bear witness to these mistress-marks as they appear to-day. What a profusion still of purple robes and costly jewels! When the first American Cardinal was created, the infection of "cardinal red" seized on fashionable circles throughout the land, far and wide, ladies' bonnets and dresses fairly blushing with it, till society seemed streaked through and through with the hues of the scarlet woman, as when a blood-clot falls into an urn of water and is diffused abroad. If any say that it is only a narrow and fanciful sectarianism that can detect such minute identity between the prophetic picture and the papal reality, they have but to be reminded that so honored a Catholic saint as Beneventura condensed this whole apocalyptic prediction into a single pungent sentence, and applied it to the papacy of his day, when he designated her as "*a wanton clad in scarlet.*"

And how striking it is to note that true instinct which leads the ritualists of our time to copy the dress-marks of Rome, just as they are reviving her pagan ceremonial and doctrine,—so strongly is the prophetic negative bound to reproduce itself in every photograph of history![39]

---

[39] How the Anglican Church is "resuming the decorations of the harlot" appears from the following: In the services connected with the recent consecration of the Cathedral of Truro, the red vestments, which were abolished in the reign of Elizabeth, were again so conspicuous that *Punch* photographed the scene under the heading of "*Outbreak of Scarlatina at Truro.*" Join with this the following Church news: "Last Sunday the rector of St. Paul's Church wore a white stole embroidered in three shades of blue, the same done in monograms and flowers set with carbuncles and bugles; with Maltese crosses set with sapphires and diamonds; with lilies set with garnets,—the whole number of diamonds numbering forty, and of precious

What is that chalice which the woman lifts aloft? "*Having a golden cup in her hand, full of abominations and filthiness of her fornication.*" Idolatry and spiritual apostasy are clearly symbolized here. Concerning ancient Babylon the prophet wrote: "Babylon hath been a golden cup in the Lord's hand that made all the earth drunken; the nations are drunken with her wine, therefore the nations are mad" (Jer. li. 7).

Euphratean Babylon was the prolific mother of idolatry,—that idolatry which Scripture clearly shows to be the liturgy of demons,—and with this she seduced God's ancient people into spiritual fornication. And now the Church, having become paganized by absorbing into herself the literal elements of this ancient heathenism, is photographed as mystical Babylon, in her turn enticing to idolatry and spiritual unchastity.

It is no exaggeration to say that the Eucharistic cup which Rome now puts to the lips of her communicants, with its mixture of miracle and magic, resembles more nearly the chalice of the ancient Chaldean "Mysteries" than it does the chaste and simple memorial cup which Christ left in the hands of His Bride, the Church; and, in view of the transformation which has taken place, what startling significance is there for Romanizers in the apostle's saying: "Ye cannot drink the cup of the Lord and the cup of demons. Ye cannot be partakers of the Lord's table and the table of demons"! (1 Cor. x. 21),—startling, if indeed it be true, that the Bride of Christ, who in the beginning is described as having "*turned to God from idols* to serve the living and true God, and wait for His Son from heaven," is become such that she is now turning men from God to serve idols, seducing them to make an image of the sacrament, before which they fall down in worship.[40]

"And His name shall be in their foreheads," is the promise given to the Bride of the Lamb. And Antichrist's bride must maintain this parody, so, as the spouse of him who is "*the mystery of iniquity,*" this woman of the

---

stones one hundred and thirty-five: estimated cost of this memorial gift, £ 1,000. A visitor describes the Bishop of Lincoln as 'adorned with mitre and cloth of gold, his orphreys so lavishly decorated with amethysts, pearls, topazes, and chrysolites set in silver as fairly to dazzle the beholder.' How repulsive is all this to such as seek to maintain the simplicity that is in Christ!"

[40] "If any man shall say that this holy sacrament should not be adored, nor carried about in processions, nor held up publicly to the people to adore it, or that its worshippers are idolaters, *let him be accursed.*"—*Council of Trent.*

Apocalypse is thus presented to us: "And upon her forehead a name written," "MYSTERY, BABYLON THE GREAT, THE MOTHER OF HARLOTS AND ABOMINATIONS OF THE EARTH." Need we ask who it is that arrogates to herself the title, "Rome, Mother and Mistress?" Striking as are the parallels, even more so are the contrasts. "*Jerusalem which is above, who is the mother of us all,*" confesses the Holy Church whose citizenship is in heaven; the Church which has become earthly and idolatrous is characterized as "*Babylon the great, the mother of harlots.*" The Bride is "*arrayed in fine linen, clean and white,*" which is the "righteousness of saints." The Harlot is "*arrayed in purple and scarlet color,*" which is the vesture of kings. The union of the true Church with Christ in Heaven is a "*great mystery;*" the union of the false Church with the rulers of this world is the counter "*mystery.*"

As for that other cup with which the Harlot has intoxicated herself,—"*I saw the woman drunken with the blood of saints and with the blood of martyrs,*"—what language shall we borrow to describe it? It has been estimated that the papacy has directly or indirectly slain fifty millions of martyrs on account of their faith, the vast majority of these being sincere Christians, whose only crime was that they would not own allegiance to Antichrist. Let charity discount the number by one half, if it were possible, and let her suggest every conceivable palliation for the murder of the rest, and we still have the most ghastly chapter which the volume of history contains. Would that we might mingle our weeping with floods of repentant tears from the eyes of this cruel mother, if, forsooth, we could thereby mitigate the wrath treasured up against the day of wrath which her crimes have earned. But, alas! we find "*Te Deums*" sung over Huguenot slaughters, but not one papal *Miserere* can we discover. Commemorative medals are still extant signalizing the massacre of St. Bartholomew, but not one *monumentum lacrimarum* over that event is to be found in all the archives of the seven-hilled city. "And when I saw her *I wondered with great wonder,*" writes the Seer; and now that history has filled in every detail of the crimson outline of prophecy, we wonder with even profounder amazement that such a demoniacal tragedy could ever have been enacted in the name of Christianity. But we remember that the woman who did these things was "drunken." And there is no intoxication so profound as that induced by pagan superstition tinctured with Christian blood. Even Martin Luther, while yet in the delirium tremens of popery, raged with this blood-thirst. "So intoxicated was I, and drenched in papal dogmas," are his words, "that I would have been most ready to murder, or assist others in murdering, any person who should have uttered a syllable against the duty of obedience to the Pope." Nay, even those who have been sobered by generations of Protestant abstinence from persecution, if they once return to the cups of the Harlot, speedily exhibit symptoms of the old appetite, as witnessed, for example, in the oft-quoted saying of Dr. Manning, now cardinal, when urging Romish aggression in England: "It is yours, right reverend fathers, to subjugate and subdue, to bend and to break the will of an imperial race."

This mystical name of "*Babylon the Great*" is marvellously apt on many grounds. It was literal Babylon that was the most constant and inveterate persecutor of ancient Israel. So was this typical Babylon to be the most malignant persecutor of spiritual Israel, the true and uncorrupted Church of Christ. This were enough to justify the analogy. But we believe that there is even a profounder significance in the name. Papal Babylon, as we have said above, was to reenact the idolatries of Chaldean Babylon to such an extent that she would be the restored image and counterpart of her. How the Babylonian *cultus* was diffused abroad among surrounding nations, and how it reappeared in the Roman Empire, and was in turn copied and reproduced by the papacy, is a matter of history. It is too great a subject to be discussed in a single chapter. The most that we can do now is to note some marks of identification between the idolatry of the mystical city and that of the literal city. Read in Jeremiah xliv. Jehovah's terrible denunciation of the Jews in Egypt for their obstinate worship of "*The Queen of Heaven.*" This was Semiramis, or Astarte, the great Babylonian goddess. She was called "the mother of the gods," and was "most worshipped of all the divinities." In the corruptions of Christianity, the Virgin Mary, astonishing to tell, was gradually lifted into her place, and adored under the identical titles, till to-day the voice of the papacy is exactly that of apostate Israel: "But we will certainly do whatsoever thing goeth forth out of our own mouth to burn incense unto the queen of heaven" (Jer. xliv. 17). Not only incense, but, these same Jews confessed, "we did *make our cakes to worship her*" (v. 19). Here the pedigree of the wafer is suggested; and if one will candidly trace back the descent, we challenge him to resist the conclusion that the wafer comes from the

Babylonish cake, its roundness being due to the fact that it was originally an image of the sun, and worshipped as such. Consider, also, the use, in worship, of candles, which the ritualists are now so sedulously employing to light themselves back into the Dark Ages. In the apocryphal book of Baruch there is a minute and extended description of the Babylonish worship, with all its dark and abominable accessories. Of the gods which they set up in their temples, it is said that their "eyes be full of dust through the feet of them that come in." And then it is added that the worshippers "*light for them candles, yea, more than for themselves, whereof they cannot see one.*" In the pagan worship at Rome, which was confessedly borrowed largely from Assyria and Egypt, we have accounts of processionals, in which surpliced priests marched with wax candles in their hands, carrying the images of their gods; and we find a Christian writer, Lactantius, A. D. 260-330, ridiculing the heathen custom of lighting candles to their gods, "because they are of the earth, and stand in need of lights that they may not be in darkness," which he certainly would not have done had the practice formed any part of primitive Christian worship.[41] And time would fail to tell of the confessional, so closely reproducing that imposed on the initiates in the ancient mysteries; and of holy water, of the eastward posture, of the signing with the cross, and of ceremonies and vestments, nameless and incomprehensible. Granting, for the sake of charity, that altars and incense were borrowed from Jewish worship,—which things, indeed, were done away in Christ,—it still remains true that the great bulk of the papal ceremonies were originally part and portion of primitive idol-worship, of which idol-worship Babylon was the chief mother and nurse.[42]

The complete image, as presented in this vision, is one of the most striking in all prophecy. "*And I saw a woman sit upon a scarlet-colored beast,*"—the apostate Church riding upon the state, supported by it, and yet controlling it. Who does not know how exactly this harmonizes with the facts; how the Church, upon her fall, saddled herself upon the empire, till, acquiring

---

[41] *Divine Institutes*, b. vi. 2. Bishop Coxe, the High Church editor of the American edition of the Fathers, gives this note on this passage: "The ritual use of lights was unknown to the primitive Christians, however harmless it may be."

[42] For a profound and learned exhibition of this whole subject see Hislop's "*Two Babylons,*" London, S. W. Partridge & Co.

complete control, she became able to hold it in by bit and bridle of bull and concordat, compelling it to bear her weight and to do her will? Blasphemy and apostasy are counterparts. Antichrist, a world-king, sitteth in the temple of God, showing himself as God. Antichurch, forfeiting her citizenship in heaven, now sitteth in the seat of kings. "Simeon and Levi are brethren: instruments of cruelty are in their habitations. O my soul! come not into their secret." "*Upon a scarlet-colored beast,*"—predictive of blood-guiltiness, a foreview which history has amply verified. "Grind enough of the red," used to be the ghastly phrase of the painter David, one of the French revolutionists, as he urged on the bloody work of the guillotine. Rome secular has never been sparing of the red in carrying out the orders of Rome spiritual, whom she has faithfully served as public executioner; she has painted true to the prophetic pattern. Hence the "names of blasphemy" which cover her. With heaven-defying self-exaltation she has assumed to sit in the judgment-seat of God, and to condemn His saints by millions to death, so that whereas Jehovah was wont to reprove kings for their sakes, saying, "Touch not my anointed, and do my prophets no harm," these—the Harlot and the Hierarch—have "taken counsel together against the Lord and against His anointed," to burn them at the stake and rend them in the Inquisition. And yet, after all, the longing is irresistible, that this fallen daughter of God—the harlot Church—might be reformed, and like that other Magdalene be found bathing the Saviour's feet with her penitent tears. Nothing in history is more pathetic than that yearning of pious Catholics of the Middle Ages which found expression in the prophecy of a "*Papa Angelicas,*" about to appear, an Angel-Pope, who should restore the denied Church to her primitive purity, and invest her once more with the white robes of spiritual chastity. But such a conception is as contrary to possibility as it is counter to Scripture. That which has been the curse of the Church can never be its cure. An angelic man in the papal chair, if such an one could be found to sit there, would be as abhorrent in his office as he might be lovely in his person, for papacy is the essence of Antichrist, and as such can never help Christ in reforming His Church. If any demur at this, and contend that with all her errors Rome still holds enough of truth to constitute her a true Church, we must reply that she cannot be both the bride and the harlot; and to this her most eminent prelates assent, compelling us to choose between the two alternatives. Cardinal Manning says: "*The Catholic Church is either the masterpiece of Satan or the Kingdom of the Son of God.*"[43] We solemnly deny that she is the latter. Cardinal Newman declares: "*Either the Church of Rome is the house of God or the house of Satan: there is no middle ground between them.*"[44] We solemnly affirm that she is not the former.

And yet the cup of the Roman sorceress, let us remember, is once more put to the lips of Protestants, who are solicited to drink it, and forget their estrangement from their "Mother Church." How many have been drugged into communion, or at least into wanton dalliance, with her, we need not say. It is enough to utter the warning, that here fellowship is fornication. If, by the regenerating and sanctifying grace of the Spirit, we belong to the true body of Christ, we are bound to meet every overture for communion with Rome with the inspired question and inspired answer of the apostle: "Shall I, then, take the members of Christ, and make them members of a harlot? God forbid" (1 Cor. vi. 15).

---

[43] *Lectures on the Fourfold Sovereignty of God*, London, 1871, p. 171.
[44] Essays, ii. p. 116.

V.
THE MOCK MILLENNIUM.

ANTICHRIST and Antichurch,—these two reigning together have brought on an anti-millennium, the dazzling caricature of that which is promised to appear at the second coming of Christ and the marriage of the Lamb. An eminent exegete, in a recent symposium on the pre-millennial advent, replies to those who query whether the present may not after all be the long-predicted millennium, that it might be more correctly called "the millennium of Satan." This saying sounds extremely harsh and pessimistic, but it has the advantage of conforming to Scripture. "The age to come"—ὁ αἰὼν μέλλων—has its unmistakable characteristics as set forth in Scripture: it will be the age of the resurrection of the just (Luke xx. 35), with all the glorious triumphs and rewards which belong to that consummation; and it will be ushered in by the visible appearing of the Lord from heaven (Matt. xiii. 39); it will be Christ's millennium, during which Satan shall be bound and shut up so that he can tempt the nations no more (Rev. xx. 1-5).

The present age,—ὁ νῦν αἰών,—spanning the entire distance from the first to the second advent, has also its distinctive characteristics: it is called "the present evil age" (Gal. i. 4); Christians are exhorted to "live soberly, righteously, and godly in this present age" (Titus ii. 12), to "be not conformed to this age" (Rom. xii. 2), and they are admonished that Christ "gave Himself for our sins, that He might deliver us from this present evil age" (Gal. i. 4). So far from Christ being Lord of this age, as He should be were it His millennium, we are distinctly told that Satan is "the god of this age,"—ὁ θεὸς τοῦ αἰῶνος τούτου (2 Cor. iv. 4). Till this dispensation ends, therefore, and the sway of its god is broken, there can be no millennium of universal righteousness in which Christ shall reign with His saints upon the earth. Multitudes will be *taken out of this age* to form the *Ecclesia*, the called out, the Bride of Christ, to be presented to Him at His coming; but the Church will never so transform the dispensation as to turn it into a blissful millennium. The clock of the ages runs true to the eternal order, and however impatient the Church may be for the consummation of all things, she cannot move forward the hands of that clock a single hour to bring in the Sabbatic rest before the fulness of time be come. But this was really what was attempted by the Church after her elevation to an earthly throne under Constantine. She grasped for her glory in the time appointed for her humiliation, and vainly thought to reign in the earth while her King is still absent in heaven.

With the historical school of interpreters we find in the twelfth chapter of Revelation a graphic portraiture of this critical era. The sun-clothed woman figures the Church in her investiture with rule and authority under Constantine; her travailing and bringing forth the man child who was "to rule all nations with a rod of iron," exhibits her compassing earthly dominion and sovereignty, which dominion and sovereignty are, however, caught away from the true Church, whose portion is for the present the wilderness and rejection, and reserved with Jesus Christ on the throne where He is "expecting till His foes be made His footstool," when the promise shall be fulfilled to Him and to His reigning Bride: "I will give thee nations for thine inheritance, and for thy possession the ends of the earth. Thou shalt break them with a rod of iron, like a potter's vessel shalt thou dash them in pieces." But in the conflict between paganism and Christianity, in which the former is overthrown, as symbolized by the casting out of the dragon, the deluded Church imagines that her millennial triumph has arrived, and the cry is heard: "Now is come salvation and strength, *and the kingdom of our God and the power of His Christ*" (Rev. xii. 10). Mr. Pember, though not following this interpretation of the Apocalypse, has most admirably sketched its historical counterpart. He says: "When the Christians were relieved from persecution by the policy of Constantine, and came into honor after having been so long reckoned as the filth of the world and the offscouring of all things, the cry was straightway raised that the kingdom had come. But the result of this vain Lo here! was the introduction of two pernicious doctrines, that the kingdom is possible without the personal presence of the King, and that the Church can become mistress of the world during her widowhood and while Satan is still reigning prince. Further mischief followed, for there being nothing to support such views in the New Testament, those who entertained them were compelled to have recourse to the Old, and to cite from thence the prophecies of Israel's future glory, in order that by a false application of them to the Church they might justify the prosperity which had accrued to her through her alliance with the pagan world."[45]

Satan, who is the god of this age, is an anti-god, and as such he is the great caricaturist of all holy persons and things, that he may the more effectually delude and destroy. And having seen the counter Christ and the counter Church which he created for leading men astray, we shall now consider how through these two he brought in a counter millennium, an astonishing parody of the true Sabbatic era and the real kingdom of God on earth which are promised in connection with Christ's second advent.

Everything which belongs to that blessed age has been, and is still, claimed by the apostate Church as already here. Was not Christ to usher in the millennium by His personal coming? "On thee, most blessed Leo, we have fixed our hopes as the Saviour that was to come,"—"*Salvatorem venturum.*"[46] So spake an adoring bishop to the pope at the fifth Lateran council. In his sovereign vicar, Christ has already appeared and is already ruling, says Rome. "In the person of Pius IX., Jesus reigns on earth," exclaims Cardinal Manning, "and he must reign till He hath put all enemies under His feet!"[47]

But was it not appointed to the Church to suffer with Christ during this dispensation, that she might reign with Him in the age to come? "Nay, but now is come salvation and the kingdom of our God," replies the harlot bride. Hear the Bishop of Medrusium at the fifth Lateran council again: "But weep not, daughter of Zion, for God hath raised up a Saviour for thee; *the Lion of the tribe of Judah* (alluding to Pope Leo), the root of David hath come, and shall save thee from all thy enemies."[48] A "little flock" waiting for "the Chief Shepherd" to appear; an espoused bride looking for the Bridegroom's return,—such we had supposed to be the character of the Church in this present time. But the unfaithful spouse has found her Chief Shepherd and Bridegroom in the pope. Marcellus, in behalf of the Church, speaks thus to

---

[45] *Antichrist, Babylon, and the Coming Kingdom*, p. 145.

[46] Harduin, 1651.

[47] See closing pages of *Vatican Council*, by Henry Edward, Archbishop of Westminster, 1871. It is an exaltation of the pope as "the supreme judge and infallible teacher of men," ending with a warning to his enemies that "whosoever shall fall on this stone shall be broken, but on whomsoever it shall fall it will grind him to powder." It is an amazing exhibition of eloquent blasphemy.

[48] Harduin, 1687.

Leo X.: "I come to thee as my *true Lord and Husband*, beseeching thee to look to it that thy bride may be renewed in her beauty; and see to it that the flock committed to thee be nourished with the best and spiritual aliment, the fold united in one which is now divided, and the sickness healed which has afflicted the whole world: for thou art our *Shepherd, our Physician, our Governor, in fine, a second God on earth.*"[49]

Christ foretold the condition of his true Church—"the children of the bride-chamber"—during His absence thus: "But the days will come when the Bridegroom shall be taken from them, and then shall they fast." The Church of this false kingdom, this pseudo-millennium, is thus pictured in the Apocalypse: "*For she saith in her heart, I sit as queen and am no widow, and shall see no sorrow*" (Rev. xviii. 7). How literally was this prediction translated into history when the infatuated Eusebius, glorying over the triumphs of Christianity in his day, exclaimed: "Whereas the Church was widowed and desolate, her children have now to exclaim to her: 'Make room! Enlarge thy borders! the place is too strait for us.' The promise is fulfilling in her: 'In righteousness shalt thou be established; all thy children shall be taught of God, and great shall be the peace of thy children.'" Nay, more: so far from fasting, and waiting the time when they should sit down with the Lord at His table in His kingdom, this historian rejoices that after the enthronement of Christianity under Constantine, when "the bishops sat down at the emperor's table, and the rest all around him, it *looked like the image of the very kingdom of God.*"[50]

Though "a name above every name" is given to Immanuel, He still waits for every knee to bow to Him; He still waits for His promised throne, "the throne of His father, David." He still waits for His royal title, "King of kings and Lord of lords," which title, as the Scripture shows, belongs only to the day of His glorious coming. But not so with Antichrist. "There is but one name in the world," he declares, "and that is the pope; he only can use the ornaments of empire; all princes ought to kiss his feet; he alone can nominate and displace bishops, and assemble and dissolve councils. Nobody can judge him; his mere election constitutes him a saint; he has never erred, and never shall err in time

---

[49] Harduin, 1687.
[50] V. C. iii. 15.

to come; he can depose princes, and relieve subjects from their oaths of fidelity."[51]

What wonder that with such assumptions all the sublime promises of the millennial glory should have been counted as now fulfilled! So it was; and we read of the ambassadors of the Portuguese king bowing down to Pope Leo, and, after addressing him as "*Supreme Lord of all,*" blasphemously adapting to him the words of prophecy: "Thou shalt rule from sea to sea, and from the river *Tiber* to the ends of the earth; the kings of Arabia and Saba shall bring gifts to thee; yea, all princes shall worship thee, all nations shall serve thee."

At no point has the Messianic glory been more brilliantly mimicked than here. The profusion of offerings which have poured in upon the royal priest of Rome from the kings of the earth is astonishing to recount. No monarch that ever reigned has been the recipient of such sumptuous gifts from the princes of this world. And the spell of fascination which has ever evoked such tributes, although long weakened, seems to be again reviving, as indicated by the published list of royal presents to the pope on his recent jubilee. The soft adulation toward Rome, which many Protestant clergymen have learned to cultivate during the last half century, is now being matched by a renewed subserviency on the part of kings. Bishop Cox, one of the compilers of the Liturgy of the Anglican Church, writing from England to friends on the Continent in 1559, while Elizabeth was reigning, said: "We are thundering forth in our pulpits, and especially before our Queen Elizabeth, that the Roman Pontiff is truly Antichrist." Such thunder has so far subsided among those employing this liturgy that now a great company of priests are laboring to bring about organic union with Rome, and the present successor to Elizabeth on the English throne sends one of the most princely of the anniversary gifts to Leo XIII. Luther, after his eyes, long holden of superstition, were opened to discern the Scriptures, looked at prophecy and then at the papacy and exclaimed: "It is most manifest, and without any doubt true, that the Roman Pontiff, with his whole order and kingdom, is the very Antichrist." But instead of Luther's mitre of malediction upon the head of this usurper of Christ's millennial throne, Germany now sends, as the tribute of King William to the Roman Pontiff, "a jewelled mitre costing four

---

[51] *Dict. Papæ*, Greg. VII.

thousand dollars." So the masquerade goes on before the eyes of men and angels, that the unwary may still longer be deceived, and made to believe that this is He of whom the Psalmist wrote, "The kings of Tarshish and of the isles shall bring presents; . . . yea, all kings shall fall down before Him; all nations shall serve Him." Only those can unmask these pretensions who read the Scriptures diligently, and find that He of whom this is written has this honor, which the pope has never known: "For He shall deliver the needy when he crieth; the poor also, and him that hath no helper. He shall spare the poor and the needy and shall save the souls of the needy; He shall redeem their souls from deceit and violence, and precious shall their blood be in His sight" (Psalm lxxii. 12-14).

Not merely the millennial reign, but the millennial splendors, have been snatched by the faithless bride. Sober dress becomes the widowhood of the Church; gaudy attire and jewelled fingers convict her of wantoning with earthly lovers; majestic cathedrals, hoarding boundless wealth and adorned with costly furniture, imply that she has forgotten that here she has no continuing city, but that her citizenship is in heaven, from whence she looks for her Lord. Cardinal Newman, in defending these lavish splendors of the papacy, declares that their presence "as little proves that the Church is Antichrist as that any king's court is Antichrist," and then cites the following passages in their justification: "I will lay thy stones with fair colors, and thy foundations with *sapphires*, and I will make thy windows of agates, and thy gates of carbuncles, and all thy borders of *precious stones*." "The glory of Lebanon shall come unto thee, the fir tree, the pine tree, and the box together, to *beautify the place of my sanctuary*."[52] But this is only a piracy of Messianic prophecies, all these texts being descriptive of the age of glory yet to come. To quote them in this connection is simply to justify our charge that the apostasy has ravished the Church millennial to get building materials for the Church militant. It should be soon enough to walk on golden streets when the New Jerusalem descends from heaven "as a Bride adorned for her Husband;" but the harlot must needs seize the paving-stones of the Holy City to beautify the streets of "that great city which is spiritually called Sodom and Egypt, where also our Lord was crucified" (Rev. xi. 8).

---

[52] *Essays*, ii. 184.

Let it not be implied that we should be so shut up to sackcloth and ashes in the dispensation that now is, that we can have no happy glimpses of that which is to follow. Most expressively does the apostle, in the Epistle to the Hebrews, speak of Christians as those who have "*tasted the powers of the age to come*" (Heb. vi. 5). Foretastes are graciously permitted, but immediate and full appropriation is forbidden. "Be not conformed to this age, but be ye *transfigured* by the renewing of your mind," says the Scripture. The transfiguration was a prelibation of the age to come; the cup of glory tasted for a moment by our Lord to strengthen Him to drink the cup of His vicarious anguish. But it could be only a taste as yet, not a complete fruition. Yet Simon Peter, whose mistakes are always significant as foretypical of the permanent errors of his self-styled successors, exclaims, "*Let us make three tabernacles*, one for thee, and one for Moses, and one for Elias, *not knowing what he said*" (Matt. xvii. 4). As though a momentary visitation of the coming glory could now be prolonged into a residence! As though this foretaste of the millennium could be made a permanent repast! In his epistles, however, the same apostle three times speaks of "*the sufferings of Christ and the glory that should follow*," showing how clearly now the succession and characteristics of the ages had been revealed to him by the Spirit. We are still in the dispensation of Christ's sufferings; and if we have the patience of the waiting bride we shall covet no richly adorned dwellings until the dispensation of glory shall be ushered in and the word of prophecy be fulfilled: "Behold the tabernacle of God is with men" (Rev. xxi. 3).

Not only did the Church preempt the glories of the age to come, but also its retributions. And in this her presumption exceeded all bounds. "Do ye not know that the saints shall judge the world?" asks the apostle. Well might the lowly disciple of Christ be startled and staggered at such a suggestion! But it is only an illustration of the reversals which will be effected at the setting up of the kingdom of Christ. They whose portion it was to stand before the judgment-seat of kings will now sit in the judgment-seat with the King of kings, "to execute upon them the judgment written: *This honor have all his saints*" (Ps. cxlix. 9). But this exercise of judicial honor is limited most rigidly to the age to come. "Ye which have followed me, *in the regeneration*"—"in the renovation, παλιγγενεσία, being the restoration of this world of ours on the appearance of the new æon" (Lange),—"when the Son of man shall sit *on the throne of His glory*, ye also shall sit upon twelve thrones, judging the twelve tribes of Israel" (Matt. xix. 28). It is only in association with the glorified Lord, present in the body to judge men according to the deeds done in the body, that this office can be exercised by the redeemed. Therefore the Scripture is very explicit, and saith: "Judge nothing before the time *until the Lord come*" (1 Cor. iv. 5).

But see what the Church was left to do so soon as she began to glorify herself and live deliciously, and to commit fornication with the kings of the earth. She snatched both the throne and the sceptre of God, and began to deal out condemnation to His saints. The centuries of Antichrist's career have constituted one long judgment day, in which justice has been outraged as never before in the history of the ages; one prolonged assize, in which popes, and cardinals, and bishops have sat in the bench with Chief Justice Apollyon, and administered sentence according to the statutes of the Prince of Darkness.

How visibly can the form of this black magistrate be seen behind this mock tribunal; how almost audibly does the chuckle of his infernal laughter break forth over this monstrous parody of the court of God which he has seduced the apostate Church to set up! With unfathomable ingenuity he has opened, before the time, the lake of fire to which he is doomed, and made a channel for it from the apostate Church; and thus to the astonished "world-rulers of this darkness" he has shown a lurid river of the water of death proceeding out of the throne of the Beast and the Harlot, with millions of Christ's true saints writhing in its flames on account of the testimony which they bore to the faith of Jesus: fantastic cruelties burlesquing the calm justice of God; the throne of iniquity supplanting the throne of grace, and impanelling the princes of this world, who crucified the Lord of Glory, to sit in judgment upon His faithful witnesses! If we knew of no other age than this, we might verily believe that the Father of Lies had outwitted the Father of Mercies. It was the contemplation of just what we are describing that is said to have drawn forth from Voltaire the bitter remark: "If this is the best the Almighty Author can do, He deserves to be hissed rather than worshiped." No, philosopher! and we may add, no, theologian! This is not the best that God can do; this is not Christ's millennium: it is Satan's mock millennium. For some inscrutable reason, the Lord has permitted a demonstration to the principalities and powers in the heavenly places of the worst which His archenemy can do. Wait a little and the Lord shall descend from heaven to usher in the real millennium, the true Sabbatic consummation for which the ages have sighed, and for which the whole creation, until now, is groaning and travailing in pain; then our Immanuel will show us the best He can do.

It is regretted that our Protestant Christianity, in its separation from Rome, never passed entirely out of the baleful shadow of this pseudo-millennium. For many to this day confound the Church with the kingdom, and apply the promises of the glory of the age to come to the present triumphs of the gospel. God forbid that in the slightest degree we should undervalue the missionary and evangelical victories which have so signally marked this century; but if we are tempted to predict the speedy conquest of the whole world to Christ through these successes, we need to be admonished to speak according to the Word. The present is the dispensation of election; the declared purpose of preaching the gospel to the Gentiles in this age is, "*to take out of them a people for His name*" (Acts xv. 14), and it is a premature grasping of the kingdom to apply to this period those glorious predictions of universal righteousness in the age to come, with which Scripture abounds. If it be said that this conception of preaching the gospel "for a witness," and "to gather out," is a narrow and disheartening one, we reply that it is in harmony with the universal testimony of Scripture; and we shall be far safer and more successful to work according to God's schedule of the ages than according to man's time-table. Indeed, if we would be intelligent laborers for Christ, we must not fail to discriminate rigidly between the sphere of the militant Church and the sphere of the millennial Church. There is an ancient saying of great significance: "*Distinguite tempora et concordabunt scripturæ.*" "Distinguish the periods and the Scriptures will harmonize." Failure at this point has worked vast misconception. The theories of Christ's *parousia* having already occurred, of the resurrection already accomplished, and of judgment already going on in the unseen world, all rest upon that confusion of the dispensations which makes "the world to come" signify the present time or the disembodied state. Here, again, is a premature snatching of the coming glory; and to effect it the ages have been telescoped, and their distinguishing events huddled together in one promiscuous jumble. The result is, prophecy without perspective; dispensations without distances intervening; the divine vision of things to come blended with the present scene; and the whole turned into a Chinese picture, with all the objects in the foreground.

Cross-bearing, patient endurance, diligent service,—this is our present calling, while we ever pray our absent Lord "that it may please Thee shortly to accomplish the number of Thine elect and to hasten Thy kingdom." Meanwhile we are "to live soberly, righteously, and godly *in this present age,*" if by any means we may be "counted worthy *to obtain that age* and the resurrection from the dead."

VI.
THE ECLIPSE OF HOPE.

IT would be inevitable that, in the condition of things described in the previous chapter, the primitive hope of Christ's second coming in glory should pass into utter eclipse. If the Messianic reign had begun, and the kingdom had really been set up, why should Christians longer look for the Lord from heaven to establish His millennial throne? The cry, "Behold the kingdom!" now filled all mouths; the lavish splendors of the papal court dazzled all eyes; and there was little occasion for that other cry to be longer sounded,—*Behold, He cometh!"*—the cry which was first uttered by that "brother and companion in tribulation, and in the kingdom and patience of Jesus Christ," and which was continued for two hundred years by his faithful fellow-sufferers. So it was that Satan's counterfeit drove the genuine coin out of circulation, till the early advent hope of the Church passed into almost complete oblivion.

Harnack, in his masterly article on the Millennium, shows that Augustine was the first theologian "to grasp and elaborate the idea that the Church is the kingdom of Christ and the city of God; . . . that the millennial kingdom had commenced with the appearing of Christ, and was, therefore, an accomplished fact." And he adds that, "by this doctrine of Augustine's, the old millenarianism, though not completely extirpated, was at least banished from the realm of the dogmatic.[53]

Of course, as the papacy developed more and more subsequent to Augustine's day, more and more was the millennial hope of the Church obscured. For that hope stands in direct antagonism to every principle of the Hierarchy. As a learned writer has said: "It never pleased, but always gave offense to, the Church of Rome, because it did not suit that scheme of Christianity which they have drawn. The Apocalypse of John supposed the true Church under hardships and persecutions; but the Church of Rome,

---

[53] The article, "Millennium," by Prof. Adolph Harnack, of Berlin, to which we constantly refer in this chapter, is in the last edition of the *Encyclopædia Britannica*. It is the ablest exhibition, in brief compass, of the primitive and historical claims of pre-millenarianism, and of the causes of the Church's decline therefrom, with which we are acquainted.

supposing Christ reigns already by His vicar the pope, hath been in prosperity and greatness, and the commanding Church in Christendom for a long time. This has made the Church of Rome always have an ill eye upon this doctrine, because it seemed to have an ill eye upon her; and, as she grew in splendor and greatness, she eclipsed and obscured it more and more, so that it would have been lost out of the world as an obsolete error if it had not been revived by some at the Reformation."[54]

It is most striking to observe how, as the apostasy went on, not only the teaching on this subject ceased, but the symbols, and worship, and ordinances of the Church became so changed as to silence their testimony to Christ's second coming, and to throw that doctrine into eclipse.

The seduction of the Church from its primitive simplicity was accomplished mainly by these two influences: pagan philosophy corrupting her doctrine, and pagan ceremonies corrupting her worship. Both of these were inherently hostile to the chaste and artless Chiliasm of the apostolic age. The primitive hope was intolerable to rational theology, because it could not be surveyed and mapped out upon its logic charts. Hence, no sooner had philosophy been installed in the apostle's chair than it began to wage war upon the apostle's doctrine.

As the Apocalypse was regarded as the stronghold of millenarianism, determined siege was made against this book: its authority was questioned, its value discounted, till it was finally driven from the canon; and, so far as the Greek Church was concerned, it was denied a place in Holy Scripture for centuries, and consequently "Chiliasm remained in its grave."[55]

Nor was this the worst injury emanating from this source. Pagan philosophy infused its own notions of a future life into ecclesiastical theology. It deftly substituted the Platonic doctrine of the immortality of the soul for the Christian doctrine of the resurrection of the body. In harmony with this change

---

[54] Thomas Burnet, 1635-1700.

[55] Professor Harnack, avowing that millenarianism "was in former times associated—to all appearance inseparably associated—with the gospel itself," adds that "*it can only exist along with the unsophisticated faith of the early Christians*," that "the millenarians of the ancient Church, just because they were millenarians, despised dogmatic in the sense of philosophic theology." Professor Van Oosterzee also observes that there is an irreconcilable "inner discrepancy between the modern theological philosophy and the prophetic and apostolical Scriptures."—*Person and Work of the Redeemer,* p. 450.

came in the notion of judgment being administered immediately after death in the disembodied state, instead of being reserved till the coming of the Lord and the raising of the dead,—a conception as characteristic of all heathen religions as it is foreign to the teaching of both the Old Testament and the New. This eschatology of the under-world, which even to this day so deeply colors our theology, could not fail to make strongly against the original advent faith of the Church. For it changed the up-look of primitive Christianity to the down-look of pagan mythology, by making death the object of consideration instead of the coming of Christ. This was the master-stroke of Satanic art,—the substitution of death for life, of mortality for resurrection, in the hopes of the Church. It is a perversion so radical and subtle that to this day many Christians are blinded by it, so that they imagine that their dying means the same thing as Christ's coming. Twin counterfeits of paganism are these two; ritualism corrupting the liturgy of the Church with demon-worship, and Platonism corrupting the eschatology of the Church with death-worship. Instead of the expectation being fixed upon Christ's advent, it became fixed upon the soul's exit; death was glorified into a good angel; and thus mortality, Satan's masterpiece, supplanted resurrection, Christ's masterpiece, and the "Terrible Captain Sepulchre and his Standard-bearer Corruption" were crowned and throned in the place of the Coming Christ, who is "the Resurrection and the Life." In the gospel, death is made neither the *terminus ad quem* nor the *terminus a quo*, that towards which we look for the consummation of our hopes, or from which we enter upon our complete sanctification and final perfection. "Not that we would be unclothed, but clothed upon, that mortality might be swallowed up of life," is the inspired confession of the believer. And nothing will so completely quench the candle of our true hope as the opposite idea that death is the supreme deliverer to be waited for.

The ceremonies which gradually grew up in the Church tended to the same result. For as worship more and more took the place of the Word in the Christian assembly, the contemplation was withdrawn from the glories of the age to come. Purgatory was substituted for Paradise; masses for the disembodied souls in the former supplanted scriptural exhortations to the attainment of the rewards and glories of the latter. The lamp of prophecy, which the Lord left in the hands of his waiting Bride, had at last been exchanged for the tapers of heathenism. "We almost see the ceremonial of the

Gentiles introduced into the Church under pretense of religion," exclaims Jerome, "piles of candles lighted while yet the sun is shining. Great honor do such persons render to the blessed martyrs, thinking with miserable tapers to illuminate those whom the Lamb in the midst of the throne shines upon with the splendor of His majesty."[56] It will be seen from this saying which way the candle of paganism throws its beams, as compared with the true light which Christ gave to His Church. "We have also a more sure word of prophecy," writes Peter, "whereunto ye do well that ye take heed, as unto a light that shineth in a dark place, *until the day dawn and the day-star arise in your hearts.*" Here is the lamp which amid earth's night was to shed its rays far on towards the coming King, to meet and mingle with the light of His returning glory, "until the day break and the shadows flee away." What a blow was it to the bridal hopes of the Church when ceremony took the place of scriptural preaching and exposition in the assemblies of Christians!

Observe the same suppression of primitive teaching in the Christian ordinances. Baptism, as instituted by our Lord, bore graphic witness to the first resurrection, and hence at every administration it uttered a visible "Behold he cometh!" Hear the apostolic exposition of this ordinance: "Know ye not that so many of us as were baptized into Jesus Christ were baptized into His death? Therefore we are buried with Him by baptism into death, that *like as Christ was raised up from the dead by the glory of the Father, even so we also should walk in newness of life* (Rom. vi. 4): a text which shows, says Canon Westcott, that the very entrance of the primitive Christians into the Church "was apprehended under the form of a resurrection." But as the rite became mutilated in the Western Church, the tongue with which it once proclaimed our advent hope was plucked out, and its testimony silenced, so that, as now widely practiced, the ordinance gives no suggestion of resurrection.[57]

---

[56] *Adv. Vigilantium*, c. ii.

[57] Dean Stanley declares that the change from the primitive form of immersion to sprinkling has "*set aside the larger part of the apostolic language regarding baptism, and altered the very meaning thereof*" (*Essay on Baptism*). Dean Goulburn, regretting that immersion, which is the rule of his church, has been discontinued, says that, were it still practiced, "The water closing over the entire person would then preach of the grave which yawns for every child of Adam, and which one day will engulf us all in its drear abyss. But that abyss will be the womb and seed-plot of a new life. Animation having been for one instant

The Lord's Supper, also, was not only robbed of its millennial witness, but made to express a completely contrary idea. For gradually the doctrine of "the real presence" became associated with the communion. Originally the eucharist proclaimed *the real absence of the Lord.*—"*This do in remembrance of Me*" was its voice. We do not remember a present friend, but one who is absent. "For as often as ye eat this bread and drink this cup, ye do show the Lord's death *until He come.*"—We do not wait the coming of one who is with us, but of one who is away from us. The Jews to this day keep a vacant seat for Elijah at their paschal meal, remembering the word of the Lord, "Behold I will send you Elijah the prophet before the coming of the great and dreadful day of the Lord," thus making the feast anticipative as well as commemorative. And while the Bridegroom tarries, there is ever a vacant seat at the Lord's table, left empty for the Lord Himself, who distinctly said at the beginning that He would not henceforth participate in the cup with His disciples till He should drink it new with them in the Father's kingdom. Of course, in the person of the unseen Holy Spirit, Christ is ever with His Church. But visibly and corporeally He is not present; and the communion was ordained to proclaim this fact through all the interim from His departure to His return. Alas! it was a sad blow to the Church's advent hope when these two sacramental witnesses to our Lord's return were brought into a conspiracy of silence concerning that blessed event, while one of them was made to bear false testimony, proclaiming a literal presence of the Lord in body and blood, thus hushing into silence the "*until He come*" which the ordinance was originally commissioned to utter.

Thus was Christ's prophecy literally fulfilled: "While the Bridegroom tarried *they all slumbered and slept.*" And it was fulfilled exactly as the language signifies. For the word translated "slumbered" is νυστάζω, to nod. At first there were faithful witnesses, such as Nepos, Methodius, Apollinaris, and Lactantius, who sought to rouse the lethargic Church, but there was only a momentary awakening, followed by a deeper relapse into slumber. The Church drowsed and nodded, then fell into a profound sleep; and during the long period of the Dark Ages the advent faith disappeared. Not utterly, indeed, for in Harnack's expressive phrase, "It still lived on in the lower strata of Christian society; and in

---

suspended beneath the water,—a type this of the interruption of man's energies by death,—the body is lifted up again into the air by way of expressing emblematically the new birth of resurrection."—*Bampton Lectures*, 1850, Oxford Edition, p. 18.

certain undercurrents of tradition it was transmitted from century to century." That is, while the harlot Church, including the great body of nominal Christians, became completely dead to this truth, the true Bride, the woman in the wilderness, obscure, despised, and persecuted, still cherished it in secret. Hence all through the ages we find glimmering rays from the Virgin's lamp falling here and there in the surrounding darkness. The Waldensian candlestick, with its motto, *"Lux in tenebris,"* threw stray beams of advent light into the encircling gloom. Read the following from the Noble Lesson, a famous treatise originating in that body about A. D. 1200: "O brethren, hear a noble lesson: we ought often to watch and be in prayer; for we see that this world is near its fall. We ought to be very careful to do good works, for we see that the end of the world is approaching."

That other band of sackcloth witnesses, the Paulicians, gave similar testimony. For while the great body of Christendom had settled down into a contented earthly citizenship, these hunted and hated Protestants saluted each other as συνέκδημοι,—"*Fellow-exiles*," and while the blind virgin-worshipers adored the Mother of God, these spoke of the Jerusalem above, the Mother of us all, as that from whence Christ, the "Forerunner, having for us entered," would surely come again. Even from within the Catholic communion came stray testimonies, like that of Bernard of Cluny in the twelfth century:—

> "The world is very evil.
>   The times are waxing late.
> Be sober and keep vigil.
>   The Judge is at the gate."

But these were only broken rays, feeble heart-reflections from those who had kept sight of "The Bright and Morning Star," in the midnight of the Church's apostasy. We do not forget that there were powerful outbreaks of expectation of Christ's return, like that which marked the dawn of the thousandth year of the Christian era. But the conception which characterized these was that of a Judge coming in terror, not of a Bridegroom returning to bring joy to his waiting Bride. The patience of hope revived only in a panic of fear. The forebodings of this period having passed, Christendom relapsed once more into profound slumber concerning her primitive hope,—a slumber disturbed only here and there by the dreams of those whom she counted visionaries and fanatics. So it continued till the dawn of the Reformation.

PART III.

FULFILLED.

"With the Lord's second advent will begin the real reign of God upon earth—a kingdom of righteousness, holiness, and peace, consisting of saints, with exemption from the Evil One and his enticements, and under a mighty influence of celestial power. It is called the reign of a thousand years. Modern times have again paid attention to this doctrine of the Millennium, thus coinciding with the ancient Fathers. It is resounding, as it were, a new call: 'The Lord cometh!' Among believers, this doctrine, far removed from carnal conceptions, should no more be considered an error."

JOHN FREDERICK MEYER.

I.
HOPE REVIVED.

THE Reformation was virtually a republication of the gospel; it was the Christian era beginning anew, and repeating in substance the primitive features of the religion of Jesus.

The historical school of interpreters have found in the tenth chapter of Revelation a graphic and powerful prefiguration of this event: "And I saw another mighty angel come down from heaven clothed with a cloud; and a rainbow was upon his head, and his face was as it were the sun, and his feet as pillars of fire; and he had in his hand a little book open." From the description of this mighty angel we can hardly fail to identify him with the glorified Christ, the Angel of the Covenant, as already pictured in this book (i. 13-16). There is the same countenance "as of the sun shining in his strength," the same mighty voice, and the same burning feet. The conception seems to be that of Christ appearing in history to reaffirm His testament. But that which identifies this representation most certainly to our mind is its likeness to a similar scene in the Old Testament, a point hitherto overlooked, so far as we are aware. For the keys to the Revelation are generally found in the Bible itself, events of its history being so paralleled or reproduced in the Apocalyptic imagery as to render the meaning apparent.

Now the scene of the second giving of the law, as described in Exodus, seems to be substantially rehearsed in this chapter of the Apocalypse in order to figure the second giving of the gospel. The circumstances were identical. As the tables of the law had been destroyed on account of the idolatry of Israel, so now the statutes of the gospel had been annulled by the gross idolatry of the papacy. But, God having commanded Moses to hew two tables of stone, like unto the first that were broken, the servant of God stands upon Mount Sinai holding the tables in his hand. "And the Lord descended *in the cloud*" (Ex. xxxiv. 5). So in the second giving of the gospel we behold "a mighty angel come down from heaven *clothed with a cloud.*" There is the same "proclaiming" with a loud voice in either instance. "The pillars of fire" to which the angel's feet are likened complete the identification, so that we have the pillar and the cloud in both scenes. "*Behold I make a covenant* before all thy people," says Jehovah on the mountain-top. In the Apocalypse this renewed covenant is graphically symbolized by the bow overarching the angel: "*And the rainbow was upon his head.*" Moses, with the two tables of testimony in his hand received anew from Jehovah, and the one addressed in the Apocalypse with "*the little book open,*" received from the hand of the angel,—this completes the parallel. And if we may conclude, with many commentators, that the "little book open" is the gospel restored after its long suppression by the idolatrous Church, then the verisimilitude is most striking between the restoration of the law and the restoration of the gospel.

How such truths as justification by faith blazed out anew from the reopened Testament at the Reformation is well known; and the long-lost doctrine of Christ's glorious appearing as the hope of the Church could not fail in like manner to be revived so soon as the Scriptures were unchained. We do not say that primitive Chiliasm was restored in its entirety to the creed of the Reformed Church. Attention was so much occupied with the saving truths of the gospel that its sanctifying hopes were not duly emphasized. Beside there were gross and repulsive caricatures of ancient millenarianism appearing here and there to create revulsion from the true. Satan's tares were not only sown in Christ's newly-ploughed field, but they were so rank and forward in their growth as to forestall attention, and prevent the real wheat from being recognized when it should appear. But this fact is very noticeable, that, as the features of Antichrist began to be descried in the papacy by the Reformers, the mind inevitably went forward to Him who was to destroy this Man of Sin "by the brightness of His coming." So ripe was the apostasy, so near seemed the epiphany; so developed was Antichrist, so imminent seemed the coming of Christ. Clear and intelligent were the voices that began to break forth from among the disenthralled subjects of the pontiff. "The world, without doubt,—this I do believe, and therefore say it,—draws to a close. Let us, with John, the servant of God, say in our hearts to our Saviour Christ: Come, Lord Jesus, come."[58] So spoke Ridley in 1554; and his fellow-martyr for the truth, Cranmer, said likewise: "We ask that His kingdom come, for that as yet we see not all things put under Jesus' Christ. . . . As yet Antichrist

---

[58] *Lamentation for the Change of Religion.*

is not slain. Whence it is, we desire and pray, that at length it may come to pass and be fulfilled; and that Christ alone may reign with His saints, according to the divine promise, and live and have dominion in the world according to the decrees of the Holy Gospel, and not according to the traditions and laws of men, and the will of the tyrants of this world."[59] And Hugh Latimer spoke to the same intent: "Let us therefore have a desire that this day may come quickly; let us hasten God forward; let us cry unto Him day and night, 'Most merciful Father, Thy kingdom come.' St. Paul says: 'The Lord will not come till the swerving from the faith cometh' (2 Thess. ii. 3), which thing is already done and past. Antichrist is already known throughout all the world: wherefore the day is not far off. Let us observe, for it will one day fall on our heads."[60]

These are testimonies which gleam with the light of martyr-fires already kindling upon their confessors,—fires which were sent to purify that hope which is itself the purifier of the saints. As an old coin stamped with the image of some forgotten king, but so worn by use that the royal countenance has disappeared, yet being subjected to a powerful heat gives back the obliterated face again to the beholder, so the image and superscription of the coming Christ, our advent Redeemer, long effaced from the gospel by idolatry and vain philosophy, reëmerged in the martyr-fires of the Reformation; and once more men read and repeated the words thereon: "Behold, I come quickly."

As to the other reformers, Martensen, the eminent Danish theologian, has expressed his regret that when Luther and his coadjutors, under God, set their hands to recover the primitive faith, they should not have restored apostolic millenarianism, and given it a place in the reformed creed. But Luther did not reject it, though this has been alleged. "The Jewish opinions" so pointedly condemned in the Augsburg Confession, which he assisted in drafting, really had reference to the notion of a millennium in the flesh, or the setting up of the kingdom of God in this present evil age and before the advent. Some extreme Anabaptists had exhibited this travesty of a sacred truth, and in carrying out the idea had stirred up sedition and brought scandal upon the Protestant movement. At these the disavowal was aimed.[61] The article in

---

[59] *Catechism of Edward* VI., 1533.

[60] *Sermons on the Lord's Prayer.*

[61] "And as at the time, among other calumnies, this blame was also cast upon us, as if the gospel taught and encouraged rebellion and undutifulness toward authorities, we had, by

question really condemns the post-millenarianism now so greatly in vogue among us. It reads: "They condemn others also, which spread abroad Jewish opinions, that before the resurrection of the dead, the godly shall get the sovereignty in the world, and the wicked be brought under in every place." That the godly will not get the sovereignty of the world, and subdue the wicked before the resurrection at Christ's coming, is what true Chiliasm has always avowed.

How strongly the principal reformers emphasized this view, as against the notion of world-conversion and regeneration before the advent, now so widely accepted among religious teachers, will appear from two or three quotations. "Some say," writes Luther, "that before the latter day the whole world shall become Christians. This is a falsehood forged by Satan that he might darken sound doctrine. Beware, therefore, of this delusion."[62] And John Knox, the intrepid Scotch reformer, likewise declares: "To reform the whole earth, which never was, nor yet shall be, till that righteous King and Judge appear for the restoration of all things."[63] Of the unfitness of the conception of the kingdom appearing before the King, of the triumph of the saints before the triumph of the Saviour, John Calvin thus speaks: "Christ is our Head, whose kingdom and glory have not yet appeared. If the members were to go before the Head, the order of things would be inverted and preposterous; but we shall follow our Prince then when He shall come in the glory of His Father and sit upon the throne of His majesty."[64] These selections sufficiently indicate how strongly the negative aspects of Chiliasm were maintained by the Reformers. When we hear their positive avowals of the certainty and imminence of the Lord's second advent, their position becomes even more clearly defined. Hear Knox in his letter to the faithful in London, in 1554: "Has not the Lord Jesus, in spite of Satan's malice, carried up our flesh into heaven? And shall He not return? We know that He shall return, and that with expedition." Luther in his weariness of the Reformation battle, cries out affectingly: "There is no more help or counsel upon earth except in

---

these words of the Confession, to free ourselves of such imputations."—*Melancthon's Works*, vol. xxvi., p. 366.

[62] *Com. on John*, x. 11-16.

[63] *Treatise on Fasting*.

[64] *Psychopannychia*, p. 55.

the last day. I hope, too, that it will not be much longer before it comes; I believe that the gospel will become so despised that the last day cannot be far off, not over a hundred years. God's Word will again wax less and fall off, and great darkness will come for want of true and faithful ministers of the Word. Then will the whole world run wild, sensual, and live in all security without reflecting. Then shall the voice come and sound, 'Behold, the Bridegroom cometh,' for God will not be able longer to endure it."[65]

If the excesses of certain Anabaptists prejudiced Luther and his associates so that they did not give millenarianism that recognition in the reformed theology which it deserved, the fidelity of others of this sect—"many of whom," says Harnack, "need not shun comparison with the Christians of the apostolic and post-apostolic ages"—had much to do with keeping it alive in Christendom. This, Harnack distinctly recognizes, declaring that, while the Reformers followed too much the teachings on this subject which had prevailed in the Catholic Church since the time of Augustine, "millenarianism nevertheless found its way, with the help of Apocalyptic mysticism and Anabaptist influences, into the churches of the Reformation, chiefly among the reformed sects, but afterwards also into the Lutheran Church." Of these reformed sects we can only speak briefly. The lineal descendants of the Anabaptists—John Bunyan's spiritual kinsmen and fellow-sufferers in England—presented a confession to Charles II. which embodies "the purest early Patristic millenarian doctrine of any creed in modern times." There were apostolic names among the more than twenty thousand Baptists who, in giving their adhesion to this document, declare: "We are not only resolved to suffer persecution to the loss of our goods, but also life itself, rather than decline from the same." The confession contains a touching avowal of the pilgrim condition of Christ's disciples until His advent, on which event their hopes are placed: "Though now, alas! many men be scarce content that the saints should have so much as a being among them, *but when Christ shall appear, then shall be their day: then shall be given them power over the nations to rule them with a rod of iron; then shall they receive a crown of life which no man taketh from them.*" If the Westminster Confession was less explicit so far as giving any formal expression of Chiliasm,

---

[65] *Table Talk.*

it at least sets the hope of our Lord's ever imminent return into conspicuous prominence, declaring: "Christ will have that day unknown to men, that they may shake off all carnal security and be always watchful, because they know not at what hour the Lord will come." With the Evangelical party in the Episcopal Church this has been so strong a conviction and article of faith as to render them its most conspicuous champions in modern times.

Among the fathers of Congregationalism, especially those who planted the gospel in America, the ancient doctrine was strongly held and ardently preached. New England theology was in the beginning as deeply colored with millenarian hopes as primitive Christianity itself. The Mathers, who preached in the city in which we write, and whose sepulchres are with us to this day, were bold confessors of apostolic Chiliasm; and considering how strongly other eminent men of their day echoed their sentiments, Davenport, Spaulding, and Walley, we must conclude that this precious faith had found another blooming period in connection with this eventful planting of the gospel. But, alas! as in the beginning this doctrine was wrecked on the philosophy of Augustine, so now it disappeared before the mighty logic of Jonathan Edwards. For, in his "History of Redemption," though he speaks clearly of the literal advent and resurrection, the millennial hope of God's Church is so spiritualized and attenuated as to be utterly unrecognizable; and from his day the Church, of which he was so eminent a light, has drifted more and more toward that post-millenarianism which may have had not a little influence in producing the baleful fruits of eschatology now ripening among us.

All that we can give in our brief space is only the merest outline of the *renaissance* of millenarianism. The clearest traces of the revived hope of the Church, however, appear in the noble line of Apocalyptic expositors—a true apostolic succession—beginning with Joseph Mede, born in the same half century in which Luther died, and coming down to Elliott in our own century. Their way is like the path of the just that shineth more and more unto the perfect day; in their hands the prophet's lamp glows with ever-brightening beam towards the millennial dawn. Indeed, whenever men have turned from dogmatics to Scripture, a revival of millennial views has been inevitable. So it was that when the great evangelical exegete Bengel appeared, and began to unchain the Word of God and allow it to speak for itself, such an impulse was given to advent truth that, according to Hengstenberg, "Chiliasm obtained an almost universal diffusion through the Church."[66] And yet, as ever, there were many adversaries. Of Bengel, Dorner says: "His works were the first cock-crowing of the new kind of exegesis the Church so greatly needed." But before the cock-crowing was fairly heard, the advent faith was thrice denied by the incredulous question: "Where is the sign of His coming?" For in the same century with Bengel wrote Whitby the Arian, the author of that "New Hypothesis" in eschatology called post-millennialism, which now rules so largely in the theological schools of this country,—a spiritualizing system whose ultimate tendency has been to obscure the doctrine of a literal advent, a literal resurrection, and a literal kingdom, and to put far off the day of the Lord. Just as Judaizing conceptions brought the doctrine of the millennium into disrepute in the early ages by carnalizing it, so this interpretation has tended to discount it in our times by spiritualizing it. Once more, however, has come a reaction towards the ancient teaching. For in our own generation has been witnessed such a flaming-up of the torch of primitive adventism as has not been known since the first century. The learned exegete and the humble Bible-reader—the one searching with the critical eye of scholarship, and the other with the single eye of faith—have reached the same conclusion, and joined to sound out together the cry, "Behold, He cometh!" What eminent expositors are to-day standing forth to give their bold adhesion to this much-maligned doctrine! What eloquent preachers have risen up to sound out the cry, "Behold, the Bridegroom cometh!" What ardent evangelists are going through the land bearing in their hands the relighted lamp of prophecy, opening and alleging that "this same Jesus, who was received up into heaven, shall so come in like manner as He went up!" What gifted poets have tuned their lyres to this exalted theme, so that now, "with their garlands and singing-robes about them," they are heralding with Milton, their choir-leader, "*the eternal and shortly expected King!*" What crowded assemblies are gathering for conference and mutual encouragement concerning this lofty theme! All these things constitute an undisputed sign of that greater sign, "the sign of the

---

[66] "To whom else do we owe it that the Orthodox Church of the present time does not brand the Chiliastic view of the last times as a heterodoxy, as is done in almost all the manuals of dogmatics, so that there is scarcely a believing Christian now who does not take this view?"—Delitzsch.

Son of man in heaven," coming to heed at last the sigh of groaning and travailing creation, to renew the face of the earth, that it may be to the Lord "for a name, for an everlasting sign, that shall not be cut off."

II.
FOREGLEAMS OF THE DAY.

"EUDIA!" "Fair weather!" Such is the exclamation which our Lord puts into the mouth of the watchers of the evening-red upon the western horizon; and then He chides His hearers that, discerning the face of the sky, they cannot discern the signs of the times (Matt. xvi. 2, 3). After the long, wild storm of the ages, the "hail and fire mingled with blood" devastating the earth, is it strange that we should watch eagerly for the tokens of the fair day of God which the coming of the Son of man shall usher in? Some say that signs are not for the Church, since she is heavenly, and has her home on high. But just for that reason they are for the Church, for the "strangers and pilgrims on the earth" who "desire a better country, even a heavenly."

The budding fig-tree is certainly a token for us,—a Jewish sign for the Christian Church; and if, as we believe, this phenomenon is now appearing, it should be to the waiting Bride of Immanuel as the song of her Beloved, "Rise up, my love, my fair one, and come away: for, lo! the winter is past, the rain is over and gone; the flowers appear on the earth; the time of the singing of birds is come, and the voice of the turtle is heard in the land. *The fig tree putteth forth her green figs*, and the vines with the tender grape give a good smell. Arise, my love, my fair one, and come away." The cursing of the fig tree we believe, with many expositors, to be an enacted parable. If our Lord had pointed to the green and spreading branches and said, "This is Israel," His meaning had hardly been plainer. "Leaves only,"—abundant professions, luxuriant outward religious display,—such was the character of the Hebrew Church as it appeared to the Saviour's eyes. "And he said unto it, Let no fruit grow on thee henceforward forever; and presently the fig tree withered away" (Matt. xxi. 19). Yet not forever. Why not translate the words literally, εἰς τὸν αἰῶνα, "*for the age*"? Then, in miniature symbol, we have the magnified fact to which the centuries have been bearing solemn witness, namely, that for the entire age, for the whole dispensation following their rejection of Christ, the Jewish people would be dry, and unfruitful, and dead.

But subsequently we hear our Lord saying: "Now from the fig tree learn her parable; while her branch is now become tender and putteth forth leaves, ye know that the summer is nigh." "As in its judicial unfruitfulness it emblematized the Jewish people, so here the putting forth of the fig tree from its winter dryness symbolizes the future reviviscence of that race which the Lord declares shall not pass away till all be fulfilled" (Alford, Matt. xxiv. 33). As the blight and barrenness were for the age, so the budding and blooming will be a joyful sign of the termination of the age. Thus our Lord has given one answer to the question with which this chapter opens: "What shall be the sign of Thy coming and *of the end of the age?*"

Are there any swelling buds of promise now visible on the long-withered Jewish stock? We name these, whose presence only the densest prejudice can fail to recognize as significant: The civil emancipation of Israel during the present century where in all lands she has been oppressed, as though the word of the Lord were already fulfilling, "Loose thyself from the bands of thy neck, oh, captive daughter of Zion;" the tide of emigration setting toward Palestine, accelerated of late by the persecutions in many countries, as though the Israelites were being driven out in order to be driven home; the extraordinary conquests of the gospel in later years among this people, so that it is estimated that more Jews have been converted to Christianity in the nineteenth century than during the whole period of the Christian era; and last, the wonderful Christ-believing movement headed by Joseph Rabinowitch of Russia—a movement within the Jewish Church for confessing Jesus as the Messiah—having this for its watchword: "The key of the Holy Land lies in the hand of our brother Jesus." This remarkable revival, though but five years in progress, is said to have already won to itself some fifty thousand adherents; and Professor Delitzsch, the eminent Hebraist, having studied it in the light of the prophetic Scriptures, expresses the conviction that it "marks the beginning of the end;" and with him several thoughtful Jewish Christians join in publishing their judgment, that "this movement may develop into the promised restoration of Israel."

The world-wide proclamation of the gospel is also a significant token of the approaching end of the age. "And this gospel of the kingdom," our Lord declares, "shall be preached in all the world for a witness unto all nations, and then shall come the end." Prophecy unfolds itself in concentric circles of fulfillment, each circle taking in a wider sweep of history than its predecessor, till the whole circumference of the divine prediction has been filled up. This principle is illustrated in the Saviour's saying: "Verily, I say unto you, This generation shall not pass away till all be fulfilled" (Matt. xxiv. 34). The generation then living did not pass away until the destruction of Jerusalem,—that ending of the Jewish age which was a vivid foretype of the greater event, the termination of the Christian age; but the generation in its larger sense—the Hebrew race—survived that catastrophe, and still endures, as a standing memorial of the truth of this saying of our Lord; its budding and revival to be the sure foretoken of the end of this dispensation, as its cursing and withering were of the end of the former. We may draw a figure at this point from a beautiful expression in Paul's sermon on Mars Hill, where, according to the original, he says that God hath "*horizoned* the times appointed."[67] In prophecy there are near and distant horizons, their outline so blending to the eye that they can with difficulty be distinguished. Thus do the bounds of the successive ages mingle in the outlook of the future; and, in our Lord's great eschatological discourse, so complete is the mingling that it is quite impossible entirely to separate them. Keep in mind this fact in interpreting our Saviour's prophecy of the preaching of the gospel among all nations. It was fulfilled within the narrower circle of the Roman world, before the fall of the Jewish city and the termination of the Hebrew economy. Paul, writing to the Colossians, speaks of "the gospel which is come unto you, *as it is in all the world,*" and again, of "the hope of the gospel which ye have heard, and which was *preached unto every creature which is under heaven*" (Col. i. 6, 23). The inner circle of this prediction was thus filled up; and now we wait for the outer circumference to be reached, when, in the largest sense, "all nations" shall be visited by the gospel, that the end of this dispensation may come. Need it be said that our own generation, and especially our own century, is witnessing the unquestionable marks of the fulfillment of this prediction? The century

---

[67] It is evident, comparing St. Luke with the other synoptists, that Jesus turned the thoughts of the disciples to two horizons, one near and one far off, as He suffered them to see one brief glimpse of the landscape of the future. The boundary line of either horizon marked the winding up of a æon, the συντέλεια αἰῶνος; each was a great τέλος, or ending; of each it was true that the then existing γενέα—first in its literal sense of "generation," then in its wider sense of "race "—should not pass away till all had been fulfilled. And the one was the type of the other: the judgment upon Jerusalem, followed by the establishment of the visible Church upon earth, foreshadowed the judgment of the world and the establishment of Christ's kingdom at His second coming.—Farrar's *Life of Christ*, ii. 259.

opened with almost every heathen country in gross darkness concerning the gospel; it is about to close with every nation holding up luminous points of evangelized domain to witness to God that it has received the witness of God in the gospel of His Son.

The closing words of Daniel contain another sign for us: "*But the wise shall understand.*" The book of prophecy, which was sealed "till the time of the end," was to be revealed to God's searching servants as the time of the end drew near. Therefore such uncovering of the prophetic mysteries, such inquiry and demonstration concerning the "what, and what manner of time," as our generation has witnessed, is a most striking token of the nearing termination of the age. The same Spirit who is in the Word is in the Church; and as "the testimony of Jesus is the spirit of prophecy," so the witnesses of Jesus will be the expositors of prophecy. Errors and miscalculations they will make, no doubt; but the general *consensus* of their opinion will be shaped, we believe, to the teaching of the inspired page. Therefore the deepening search is a sign of oncoming dawn. "It is not to be denied that our own age enters, with an earnestness and intensity such as no earlier one has shown, into the eschatological examination, and presses forward in the complete development of this doctrine, one sign among many that we are hastening towards the great decision."[68]

And yet this is only half a sign, the bright side of an omen of hope, whose other hemisphere is in shadow. Peter gives us the dark counterpart. "Knowing this first, that there shall come in the last days scoffers, walking after their own lusts, and saying, Where is the sign of His coming? For since the fathers fell asleep, all things continue as they were from the beginning of the creation" (2 Pet. iii. 3).[69] Language could not describe more accurately the attitude of a large section of the nominal Church respecting the future. "Evolution, not

---

[68] Kling.

[69] Never did the Church witness such a constellation of signs of the near coming of Christ as now. "The branches of the fig tree are full of sap, and the summer is at hand." Assuredly I am not ignorant that a portion of the Church has become gradually weary of the long-tarrying, and has fallen into doubt. You also shake your head, and are of the opinion that we have long talked of "the last time." Well, use this language, and increase the number of the existing signs by this new one. Add that of the foolish virgins, who, shortly before the midnight hour, maintained "the Lord would not come for a long time."—F. W. Krummacher.

catastrophe," is the cry. By the transforming power of Christian civilization, the world is to be gradually subdued to God, and the present good age, with its beneficent endowment of steam, and electricity, and printers' type, is to terminate in a Christo-scientific millennium. Darwin, the apostle of evolution, echoes back the words of Peter, the apostle of judgment, saying: "All things continue as they were since the beginning of creation; there is no need for miraculous intervention, no room for supernatural action; as it was in the beginning, so it is now, and so it shall ever be, as regards the succession of physical phenomena." In this saying he speaks for multitudes within the Christian Church. Man is the microcosm of creation; and as the doctrine of salvation by development has with many superseded that of salvation by regeneration, so has the theory of a millennium through evolution taken the place of that of a millennium, through crisis.

We should be reminded, at this point, that the signs of the approaching end of the age are both bright and dark. The gloomy pessimism which looks only for deepening apostasy is quite as wrong as the placid optimism which expects the world to glide peacefully into the golden age of glory. The brighter the light the deeper the shadow. The world-wide evangelization which our generation is witnessing; the translation of the Scriptures into innumerable tongues; the unparalleled study of the Bible, through Sunday school and lay instruction; the revivalism promoted by such bands of earnest workers of every grade and order,—these facts indicate that a light is falling upon our lost humanity such as never was before. But the shadows are "the blackness of darkness" itself. Avarice within the Church, threatening to throttle the gospel just when the promise is greatest for its triumph; anarchy without, menacing all order and stability with its angry growl; the ruin which Christian nations are sowing, in the path of the missionary's blessing, by their opium and strong drink; the ingenious vice and elaborate debauchery which our higher civilization is begetting; the restrained anger of the nations, who await only the slightest provocation to fly at each other's throats with their terrific armaments,—this outlook is so dismal as to be utterly appalling, were we not confident that even the shadows point to the dawn. "*Evil men and seducers shall wax worse and worse, deceiving and being deceived.*" Present history gives its emphatic Amen! to this sure word of prophecy. But "*the path of the just is a shining light, that shineth more and more unto the perfect day,*" and,

God be praised! a great company are walking that path to-day, with their faces brightening with a keener radiance as they behold their redemption drawing nigh. Hemispheres of hope are both, to those who know the Scriptures,—the darkness of abounding depravity, and the brightness of saintly consecration. For the energy of Satan is evermore a tribute to the zeal of God appearing in the Church. If Christians are rising up to extraordinary service for God, because they know that "the time is short," what wonder if Satan should "come down with great wrath because he knoweth he hath but a short time?"

As for chronological signs, we believe that these are given to enable us to approximate, not to calculate, the time of the end. Those computations by which some have presumed to determine the day and the hour of the Lord's return have brought great discredit upon Apocalyptic study. Only as the prophet's lamp shines upon the prophet's calendar can we read it aright; and while we examine the inspired dates of the latter, we must give heed to the divine admonition of the former: "But *of that day and hour* knoweth no man; no, not the angels of heaven, but my Father only" (Matt. xxiv. 36).

In saying this, however, we are far from disparaging the study of divine chronology. That oft-repeated interval,—"*time, and times, and a half a time,*" "*forty and two months,*" "*a thousand two hundred and threescore days,*"— we hold to signify always the same thing, according to the year-day interpretation, *twelve hundred and sixty years*. Now, as this is the period of the domination of the beast (Rev. xiii. 6), and of the witnesses prophesying in sackcloth (xi. 3), of the career of the "little horn" (Dan. vii. 24), and of the sojourn of the woman in the wilderness (Rev. xii. 6), it gives us several lines of measurement that verify each other. By general consent, the "little horn" and "the beast" signify the Antichrist. This mysterious power holds dominion for "*forty and two months,*" the same period as that of the woman's sojourn in the wilderness. But the exile of the Bride, the woman in white, must correspond in duration with the enthronement of the Harlot, the woman in purple, for these are the obverse and reverse sides of the same prophetic fact. Now, as we know from history that the Harlot has been sitting as queen on the seven hills for more than twelve hundred years, and as we know from prophecy that her opposite, the Bride, was to be in exile for "a thousand two hundred and threescore days," we conclude that these days signify years, for the Beast, and for the Bride, and for the Harlot alike, all these having the same period for their allotted career. Therefore it is not true, as some assert, that Antichrist arises only after the apostate Church has run her course, to hold sway for a literal three years and a half; but he is contemporaneous with her. Now, since Antichrist's destruction is effected by Christ's coming, the career of the former, as predicted in prophecy and confirmed by history, must furnish one of the plainest measures by which to approximate the time of the end. If the rise of the papacy could be fixed as to the exact day and year, we might not err in seeking by computation for the day and year of its fall, and so approximate closely the date of the coming of the Lord. But as its beginning was in several epoch-marking events, so, applying our measuring line, we must look for its decline in corresponding crises of decadence, each crisis being an alarm bell for admonishing us to watchfulness. From several initial dates in history, corresponding terminal periods have been correctly anticipated by students of prophecy for the last three hundred years. It is impossible to enter with detail into the subject. Nearly two hundred years ago, Apocalyptic scholars forecast the years 1790 and 1848 as critical years in the commencing of the downfall of the papacy,—the first of which, as events proved, brought her under the bloody judgments of the French Revolution, and the second into that other political convulsion which drove the pope into exile. So, likewise, many expositors concurred in looking for some marked calamity to Rome in 1868-70,—the latter year, as history was to prove, being that of the downfall of the temporal power of the pope, the severest blow, in the estimation of many, which has fallen upon Rome in a thousand years. These are illustrations of correct chronological computation which might be greatly multiplied. They suffice to indicate that they err not who, like the prophets, search "*what manner of time*" the Spirit in the Word has signified by the chronology therein given; as they suffice, also, to indicate that our century is solemnly marked as the era of expiring dates, and therefore of startling admonitions to watchful expectation.

One black, portentous cloud of warning hangs upon the horizon, to which we refer in closing. The Apocalyptic picture of the three unclean spirits like frogs, out of the mouth of the dragon, and out of the mouth of the beast, and out of the mouth of the false prophet, has been generally taken as predictive of an outbreak of sorcery. And here, as frequently, we have the divine interpretation accompanying the divine prediction: "*For they are the spirits of demons, working miracles*" (Rev. xvi. 14). It is a sign of the times not to be mistaken. The abominations of witchcraft, which God so constantly condemns in Scripture, with threat of the sorest penalties, have once more broken upon the world, under the name of Spiritualism. A great cloud of black spirits have darkened the air; millions have been seduced into lending their ears to their whisperings, and, among these, multitudes of nominal Christians. That it is "the spirits of demons" who are personating kindred and friends, and giving their soul-destroying "revelations of the unseen world," we have no question. Their fantastic miracles, their grotesque tricks of infernalism,—who has not heard of them? This we count the blackest cloud on the horizon. But observe the silver with which it is lighted up: "Behold, I come as a thief!" is the startling warning which breaks out in the very next sentence of Revelation, as though it had been said, "When you see this come to pass, then look up." And not only a warning, but an exhortation: "Blessed is he that watcheth and keepeth his garments, lest he walk naked and they see his shame." All night long the Temple watchmen made their rounds of duty, never knowing at what hour their overseer would come in upon them to learn if they were vigilant and faithful. If, coming unawares, he found any watchman sleeping at his post, the penalty was that the offender should be stripped of his garments and turned out naked of his uniform, to his shame and confusion. "Blessed are those servants whom the Lord, when He cometh, shall find watching. And if He come in the second watch, or come in the third watch, and find them so, blessed are those servants."

III.
BEHOLD HE COMETH!

IT is such a momentous event,—the coming of the Son of man in the clouds of heaven,—and the contemplation of it so overpowers the imagination, that we can easily understand why, in this age so averse to the supernatural, attempts to explain away its literalness should multiply on every hand. But, as though anticipating these evasions and refinings of latter-day philosophy, the Holy Ghost has guarded this great hope of the Church by the utmost accuracy of definition (Acts i. 11). "*This same Jesus* who is taken up from you" fixes the corporeal identity of the coming Lord with Him whom we have known of the wounded hands and pierced feet; and "*shall so come in like manner as ye have seen Him go into Heaven*" determines His literal, visible, and bodily return to earth. So, also, with the Thessalonian prediction (1 Thess. iv. 16). In the words, "*The Lord Himself* shall descend from heaven with a shout," there is a kind of underscoring of Holy Writ, that we may be particularly reminded that it is no spiritual apparition of Christ for which we look, but "His own august personal presence."

And yet His *parousia*, of which the Scripture so constantly speaks, is said to signify His presence; and therefore elaborate volumes have been written to prove that "the coming—*parousia*—of the Son of man" means His abiding invisible dwelling in the Church through the Holy Spirit. "Presence" the word undoubtedly means, but *not omnipresence*. The everywhereness of Christ in the person of the Comforter is the peculiar blessing of this dispensation. In this sense He can say to every member of His mystical body, the Church, in every place on earth and at every moment of time: "Lo, I am with you always, even unto the end of the age." It was in order to give place for this world-wide, or rather Churchwide, indwelling that it was expedient for our Lord to go away; that so the Paraclete might come to abide with His people perpetually. But this everywhere-presence of Christ by the Holy Ghost is never once spoken of in Scripture as His *parousia*. This term applies only to His bodily and visible presence, a being with us, which can only be effected by a corporeal return to us. Therefore is His advent comprehensively called His *parousia*, or coming; it is that "for which we look," and which "every eye shall see," and not that which has already come to pass spiritually, and which, therefore, no eye can see.

The second coming of Christ is the axis of a true eschatology; that in which all its doctrines and all its hopes stand together. Rightly are some insisting on what they name a Christo-centric theology; only let them consistently apply their principle to the doctrine of last things, making all our ultimate hopes and attainments to concentre in the coming Christ. Then shall we cease to hear in orthodox dogmatics that "sanctification ends at death," when the New Testament everywhere binds its consummation to the second advent of Christ; then, also, except in liberal theology, may we no longer listen to the affirmation that resurrection is attained for each one separately in an instant, in the shutting of an eye, at the last breath of the body, when Scripture declares that "*we shall all be changed, in a moment, in the twinkling of an eye, at the last trump*" (1 Cor. xv. 51, 52). Any doctrine of the resurrection dissociated from the advent must be false,—false because eccentric, and without relation to the axis of redemption, the *parousia*. No atonement apart from the cross; no resurrection apart from the coming! The morning star of the Church is the glorious appearing; but this star, at least, has satellites,—the resurrection, the rapture, the glory,—and not one of these will be visible "until the day dawn, and the day star arise."

What deep questions suggest themselves as soon as we begin to meditate on this theme! How can it be, if His coming is personal and bodily, that "*every eye shall see Him*"? Will His *parousia* be prolonged, or, as some hold, will it elapse in a moment, "as the lightning cometh out of the east, and shineth even unto the west," leaving the great world to wonder what has become of the saints? In other words, will He be visible to His Church alone at His *parousia*, manifesting Himself unto them, but not to the world until a later epiphany, when He shall appear in glory with His saints? Already there has been too much of dogmatizing on these points; therefore we prefer to leave them for the day to reveal.

The attitude of the Church towards this sublime event is the all-important consideration. That should be one of joyful hope, and not of dread expectation. We cannot think that true and watchful believers will share in that advent wail which is so graphically pictured in the Revelation (Rev. i. 7):

"All the tribes of the land shall mourn over Him," indeed, they who pierced Him reading their condemnation in His wounds and smiting on their breasts; but they who own those wounds as the credentials of their peace with God will lift up their heads and rejoice, saying: "Lo, this is our God; we have waited for Him and He will save us: this is the Lord; we have waited for Him; we will be glad and rejoice in His salvation" (Is. xxv. 9). Eagerly do we summon parable and poetry to picture the exultant scene as we gather it from Scripture. One who stands among us, as the venerable Simeon of our generation, "just and devout, waiting for the consolation of Israel,"[70] has, in a recent utterance, made the advent scene so real by the use of a historical incident, that we are constrained herewith to reproduce the picture entire:—

"When those that upheld the banner of truth had almost lost heart, and Protestantism seemed failing, John Knox accepted the invitation from the true-hearted ones, and left Geneva for Scotland. When he landed, quick as lightning the news spread abroad. The cry arose everywhere, 'John Knox has come!' Edinburgh came rushing into the streets; the old and the young, the lordly and the low, were seen mingling together in delighted expectation. All business, all common pursuits, were forsaken. The priests and friars abandoned their altars and their masses and looked out alarmed, or were seen standing by themselves, shunned like lepers. Studious men were roused from their books; mothers set down their infants and ran to inquire what had come to pass. Travelers suddenly mounted and sped into the country with the tidings, 'John Knox has come.' At every cottage door the inmates stood and clustered, wondering, as horseman after horseman cried, 'Knox has come.' Barks departing from the harbor bore up to each other at sea to tell the news. Shepherds heard the tidings as they watched their flocks upon the hills. The warders in the castle challenged the sound of quick feet approaching, and the challenge was answered, 'John Knox has come!' The whole land was moved; the whole country was stirred with a new inspiration, and the hearts of enemies withered." Oh, if that was the effect of the sudden presence of a man like ourselves,—a man whom we will rejoice to meet in the kingdom, but only a man,—what will the land feel, what will earth feel, when the news comes,

---

[70] Dr. Andrew Bonar.

"*The Son of man! The Son of man!* His sign has been seen in the heaven! O wise virgins, with what joy will you go out to meet Him!"

Some admonish us not to take too literally the words, "And at midnight there was a cry made, Behold the Bridegroom cometh!" since, sudden as the advent surprise will be, it cannot really be in the night for all the world, as one side of the globe is dark and the other light at the same moment. True; and yet how perfectly our Lord's picture of His coming answers to this fact, since it brings into the same instantaneous photograph a day-scene, and a night-scene, and a twilight-scene: "I tell you in that night there shall be two men in one bed,"—the midnight surprise; "the one shall be taken and the other shall be left." "Two women shall be grinding together,"—the twilight surprise; "the one shall be taken and the other left." "Then shall two be in the field,"—the mid-day surprise; "the one shall be taken and the other left" (Matt. xxiv. 40; Luke xvii. 34-36). It would seem thus as though the lightning-flash of His *parousia* would encircle the world in an instant. Realistic in the highest degree is the picture: no halt in the hurried march of our humanity for burnishing the armor for the grand review; no pause in life's drama for shifting the scenery before the final act is introduced! Instant transition of the Church from busy toil and tired sleep into the beatific vision and the awakening immortality, and as instant a lapse of the ungodly from the day of grace into the day of doom. The event will evidently be utterly unexpected except for the faithful few who have kept their watch.

Morally, or rather dispensationally, Christ's coming will be in the night. For such, according to Scripture, is the whole period of our Lord's absence. When He was yet with His Church He said: "I must work the works of Him that sent me *while it is day: the night cometh.*" It was His presence that made the day,—"As long as I am in the world, I am the light of the world" (John ix. 5),—and His removal that would bring the night. Hence we find Paul saying,—in the time of the Lord's absence and in view of His return,—"*The night is far spent, the day is at hand*" (Rom. xiii. 12). Here is an exact inversion of the order from that of Christ, suggesting that it is the absence or the presence of our Lord which determines the question. "*They that sleep, sleep in the night*" (1 Thess. v. 6). The words are true dispensationally as well as literally. So long as "they that sleep in Jesus" are still in their graves, the world's morning will not have come: "*And they that are drunken are drunken in the night.*" So long as the riot of unrestrained sin goes on over all the earth, and the mass of humanity is held in the mad intoxication of the god of this world, the day-dawn will not yet be visible. But what an exquisite parable there is for us—an enacted parable—in that story of Christ's walking on Tiberias! He has "gone up unto the mountain apart to pray;" and the Church which He launched is "now in the midst of the sea, tossed with waves and the wind contrary." But "in the fourth watch of the night" He comes to her, walking upon the sea; and they, who for a moment feared and were troubled at the startling apparition, will hear His voice saying, "Be of good cheer: it is I; be not afraid." These words will bring an end to all sorrow, a calm for all storms.

"And they shall see the Son of man coming in the clouds of heaven with power and great glory." Himself has said this concerning Himself, and to attempt to heighten the effect of His words by any imaginative description of the scene predicted were certainly to lower the impression which the inspired declaration itself makes upon the mind. So great is this saying that it alone befits the incarnate Word who spoke it. "Only a Jesus could forge a Jesus," it has been said; and only the Coming One whom we have known, "whose goings forth have been of old from everlasting" could predict for Himself such a coming as this. And the hope of it has reversed the current of humanity. "Man *goeth* to his long home, and the mourners go about the streets," was the plaintive strain of the old dispensation. But since Jesus ascended and put the exultant "*Ecce Venit*" into the mouth of His redeemed, "Man *cometh*" is now their song. The procession of mortality is about to halt, and then to move forward; but forward shall now signify from death to life: from the pilgrim's inn of the grave to the long home of "Forever with the Lord."

IV.
THE FIRST RESURRECTION.

THE announcement of two resurrections, separated in time by a thousand years, and distinguished in character as unto immortality and unto mortality, seems to be one of the very plainest in all Scripture: "*And I saw the souls of them that had been beheaded for the testimony of Jesus and for the Word of God: and such as worshiped not the beast, neither his image, and received not his mark upon their forehead and upon their hand: and they lived and reigned with Christ a thousand years. The rest of the dead lived not until the thousand years should be finished. This is the first resurrection*" (Rev. xx. 4, 5, R. V.). Here is first a vision of disembodied souls, then of their reanimation. This reanimation must mean a literal rising from the dead; for two words employed in the passage put the matter beyond dispute: "*They lived*"—ἔζησαν—is language which is never, in the New Testament, applied to the soul disembodied, but to man in his complete condition of body and spirit united; and "*This is the first resurrection*"—ἀνάστασις—defines this living to be bodily reanimation, since the word in the New Testament, with perhaps a single exception, always signifies corporeal resurrection. So that the phraseology employed seems to render it impossible to apply the vision either to the condition of disembodied existence or to the quickening of spiritual regeneration.

But how is it that we have never met this startling doctrine of two distinct resurrections, with a millennium between, till we reach the last book of the Bible? We have met it without being able to define it. As in Daniel, we have a condensed prophecy of the great tribulation which, by our Lord's interpretation in the twenty-fourth of Matthew, is expanded into an age-long period of Jewish trial; so in John's Gospel (v. 28), we have a miniature prediction of the resurrection: "*For the hour is coming in which all that are in their tombs shall hear the voice of the Son of God, and shall come forth, they that have done good, unto the resurrection of life; and they that have done ill, unto the resurrection of judgment,*"—which hour, in the Apocalypse of John, is interpreted as covering the entire millennial era in its fulfillment. This is according to the common method of prophecy.

Holding that the last presentation of the resurrection—this in the Apocalypse—is the completest and most comprehensive, the important question is, whether the statements of the doctrine in other parts of Scripture harmonize with this. Not only do they harmonize, but in several instances they find their only solution in it.

In the first place, we call attention to a class of passages which are marked by this peculiarity, that they seem to represent the resurrection of believers as eclectic and special. It is plain, if the scheme which we have drawn out from Rev. xx. is correct, that the subjects of the first resurrection are *called out* from the general mass of the dead; or, in other words, that a prior resurrection would involve the idea of an elect resurrection. And this conception would seem to explain at once our Lord's allusion (Luke xx. 35) to those who shall be "accounted worthy to obtain that age, *and the resurrection out from the dead*,"—τῆς ἀναστάσεως τῆς ἐκ νεκρῶν. If there be a first resurrection, at the opening of the millennial age, in which only the righteous share, the significance of this text is apparent at once. Even more striking are the words of Paul (Phil. iii. 11): "I count all things but loss . . . if by any means I might attain unto *the out-resurrection from the dead*,"— τὴν ἐξανάστασιν τὴν ἐκ νεκρῶν. The words are very strong in the Greek. We do not see how they can possibly refer to anything else than an eclectic resurrection, a separation and quickening to life out from among the dead. Especially would this seem to be so when, in addition to the very emphatic language describing the resurrection itself, there is the expression of intense desire and vehement striving to attain it. Why should one strive to attain what is inevitable, as Paul's resurrection must have certainly appeared to be, had he held that all men will be raised together? And what can our Lord's words—"They which shall be accounted worthy to obtain that age and the resurrection from the dead"—mean on any other view than that which we are defending,—the view, namely, that there is a prior age in which the rising of the saints will take place, and a distinct, and special, and privileged dispensation of bodily redemption which belongs to them? And this phase of our argument is set in very strong light by the additional fact that this expression, "resurrection from the dead,"—ἀνάστασις ἐκ νεκρῶν,—is so invariable throughout the New Testament in its application to Christ as well as to His saints. There is only one instance where the other phrase, ἀνάστασις νεκρῶν,—the general expression for *the resurrection of the dead*,—is applied to our Lord, and that seems to be on account of a special requirement of the context (Rom. i. 4.) He, coming forth from the dead, and opening the doors for all believers to come forth with Him in the resurrection unto life, is described just as they are, as rising ἐκ νεκρῶν. Hence, very significantly, we find it said in the Acts that the apostles "preached through Jesus the resurrection *from the dead*," not the resurrection of the dead (iv. 2). Now we will not dwell on the question whether the eclectic conception is contained in the words to the extent that we have claimed. We find it admitted even by some who oppose the doctrine we are advocating. Olshausen even goes so far as to declare that "*the phrase would be inexplicable if it were not derived from the idea that out of the mass of the dead some would rise first.*"[71]

And what if it be affirmed that even in the Old Testament we find distinct traces of the idea of an eclectic and precedent resurrection of the just? The passage in Daniel xii. 2, translated in our common version, "And many of them that sleep in the dust of the earth shall awake, some to everlasting life, and some to shame and everlasting contempt," is undoubtedly a Messianic prediction concerning the time of the end. Tregelles translates the passage as follows, giving us not only the authority of his own accurate scholarship for the rendering, but that of two eminent rabbis, Saadia Haggion and Eben Ezra, whose explanations are quoted at length: "And many from among the sleepers of the dust of the earth shall awake, these—that awake—shall be unto everlasting life; but those—the rest of the sleepers who do not awake at this time—shall be unto shame and everlasting contempt." Here again, if our authorities are correct, we have the idea of the first resurrection with its eclectic and separate character, and its distinct issue in life, most emphatically set forth. And how solemnly applicable to the literal as well as to the spiritual quickening of men are the words of our Lord: "The dead shall hear the voice of the Son of God, and they that hear shall live." One event awaits mankind: "Like sheep they are laid in the grave; death shall feed upon them." But all will

---

[71] "What special meaning," asks Professor Stuart, "can this language have unless it implies that there is a resurrection where the just only, and not the unjust, shall be raised?" This expression, as well as the "every man in his own order," and the evident "plain prose" character of the passage in Rev. xx., compels this learned man, though a strong post-millenarian, to concede most fully the doctrine of the first resurrection.—Stuart *on Apocalypse*, i. pp. 175, 178, 379, 499, and ii. 356, 474, 562.

not hear the great first resurrection call. As now, so then, the words of Jesus will be true: "My sheep hear my voice." As now, so then, only those that have received the spirit of adoption will cry, "Abba, Father!" as the great God shall call to the dead by the mouth of His Son. "If the Spirit of Him that raised up Jesus from the dead dwell in you, He that raised up Christ from the dead shall quicken your mortal bodies by His Spirit that dwelleth in you." That Spirit is the bond of life between Christ and all that sleep in Him, and the pledge of their redemption from the grave. The witness, now, of our sonship, He is the witness that then we shall be children of the resurrection; responding and waking instantly at the sound of the trumpet,—"Thou shalt call and I will answer;" while in "that silence that terrifies thought," the rest of the dead shall sleep on, waiting only in their conscious loss for the Day of Judgment to consummate and manifest their doom.[72]

Had we time to take up all the texts bearing on the question, we should wish to notice some passages which represent the resurrection as directly conditioned on faith and regeneration and union with Christ; all of which would go to show that the redemption of the body is a distinct inheritance of believers in some sense, and certainly not unlikely in the sense we are claiming.

We wish now to refer to two texts which have been cited as distinctly and unquestionably contradicting the theory we are advocating. The first is in 2 Timothy iv. 1, reading, according to the common version: "I charge thee, therefore, before God and the Lord Jesus Christ, who shall judge the quick and the dead at His appearing and His kingdom." It is said that we have here the living and the dead, without distinction or separation, brought together at the coming of Christ. All that need be said in regard to this passage is that, according to the revised version, the words read: "and by His appearing and kingdom." This change not only relieves the passage of any seeming

---

[72] As indicating how far this idea is from being novel or modern, we offer these striking testimonies: Chrysostom says: "The just shall rise before the wicked, that they may be first in the resurrection, not only in dignity, *but in time*" (Comment on 1 Thess. iv. 15). Jeremy Taylor says: "The resurrection shall be universal: good and bad shall rise, yet not all together, but first Christ, then they that are Christ's; and then there is another resurrection," etc. (Sermon on 1 Cor. xv. 23). Toplady says: "I am one of those *old-fashioned people* who believe the doctrine of the millennium, and that there will be two distinct resurrections of the dead: first of the just, and second of the unjust; which last resurrection of the reprobate will not commence till a thousand years after the resurrection of the elect."— *Works*, vol. iii. p. 470.

contradiction of the doctrine which we are advocating, but makes it bear emphatic support to it.

The other text is John v. 28, R. V.: "Marvel not at this; for the hour cometh in which all that are in the tombs shall hear His voice and shall come forth, they that have done good, unto the resurrection of life; and they that have done ill, unto the resurrection of judgment." This, it is said, teaches a simultaneous resurrection, since it declares that in the hour that is coming both classes will come forth to their respective rewards. We answer that, in the first place, we think it is clear that the word "hour" (ὥρα), as here employed, refers to an era or lengthened period of time. This we know is not an unusual meaning of the word, as appears by referring to such examples as 1 John ii. 18, Rom. xiii. 11; and, what is more directly to the point, our Lord had just used the term in this sense in verse twenty-fifth: "Verily, verily, I say unto you, the hour is coming, and now is, when the dead shall hear the voice of the Son of God, and they that hear shall live." This is generally taken to refer to that spiritual quickening, under the preaching of the gospel, which began with the time of Christ, and is going on to-day. Therefore the hour referred to must have continued for at least nearly two thousand years. This is the time for the quickening of the living who are dead in sins. It is evidently synchronous with 1 John ii. 18,—"It is the last time" (ὥρα),—and covers the whole gospel dispensation. Next follows, in our Lord's discourse, a statement in regard to the time of the dead. The two periods are set in contrast, as it would seem. The first—the hour of spiritual quickening—has already begun. Hence it is described thus: "The hour is coming and now is." The second had not yet begun; hence only the words, "The hour is coming," are used with reference to it. Is it not fair to presume that the second era, like the first, is a prolonged one? We think no one can reasonably deny this. This is the way we take it: At the appearing of the Lord from heaven, the age will open in which *all* that are in their graves will come forth, but some at the beginning and some at the end of the age. If it be said that it is a strained and unnatural construction to bring events which are so far apart into such immediate juxtaposition, with no intimation of any time lying between them, we reply that it is not at all uncommon in prophecy. Who, for instance, in reading Isaiah's words concerning the Messiah,—"to proclaim the acceptable year of the Lord and the day of vengeance of our God,"—would have imagined that in this single sentence two grand and distinct eras were brought together and spoken of in a breath,—the era of grace and the era of judgment? But the Lord, by His penetrating exegesis, cleft the passage asunder, we remember, as He expounded it in the synagogue, and, breaking off in the middle of the sentence,—"to preach the acceptable year of the Lord,"—He closed the book and sat down, saying: "This day is this Scripture fulfilled in your ears" (Luke iv. 21). We take it that, in this prophetic passage of His own, there is a similar conjoining of distinct and widely separated acts of the same resurrection drama.

And we are confirmed in this impression by noting how exactly this passage, with its expressions "resurrection of life" and "resurrection of judgment," corresponds to the passage in Revelation, these being common points in the two texts,—the latter seeming to fill out in detail what is here presented in outline. And this leads us to remark that there is perhaps no doctrine of Scripture the references to which are at once so fragmentary and so complemental of each other as this doctrine of two resurrections. Except in the passage in the Revelation, it is nowhere presented in a formal and complete statement. But what is very striking is, that almost every scattered allusion to it fits into this passage at some point, confirming its literal significance, and being confirmed by it. For example: All are agreed that John v. 28, 29, and Luke xx. 36, have reference to the literal rising of the body from the grave. Apply these texts to Revelation xx. 1-6, and note how perfectly they fit it: "They that have done good unto the *resurrection of life*;" "They *lived* and reigned with Christ: this is resurrection the first" (Rev.); "They that shall be accounted worthy to obtain that world and the resurrection from the dead neither marry nor are joined in marriage, *neither can they die any more*" (Luke); "On such the *second death hath no power*" (Rev.). "They that shall be *accounted worthy* to obtain the resurrection from the dead" (Luke); "*Blessed and holy* is he that hath part in the first resurrection;" "They that have done evil to the resurrection of *judgment*" [κρίσιν] (John); "And they were judged [ἐκρίθησαν] every man according to their works" (Rev.). We do not see how any candid critic can fail to identify these passages as referring to the same event, the literal resurrection of the body. And putting all these texts together, we find that one supplies what another omits; the gospels and epistles teaching the privilege and preëminence attaching to the believer's resurrection, and the Apocalypse teaching its priority and separateness in time.

Let us observe that the saints' resurrection is "first" in several senses.

It is first in time, as we have already seen. How shall we state it? That the death sentence has been shortened by a thousand years for the martyrs who have won their reprieve by their faithful sufferings for Christ; for the overcomers who have gained a seat with Christ in His millennial throne by their victory over the world. We seem to hear these sainted ones saying to grim Death, as he exacts sin's wages: "Take thy bill and sit down quickly and write fifty," for, as partners with our suffering and victorious Lord, the half of your sentence has been remitted. Of Immanuel it is written: "Whom God hath raised up, having loosed the pains of death; because it was not possible that *He should be holden of it.*" He was no prison-breaker who burst the gates of death and "tore the bars away." He had served His appointed time in the grave, and therefore could not be longer detained; and hence, after His two days' burial had expired, He received His righteous discharge. So we believe that His mystical dead body—"those that have been laid to sleep through Jesus"— cannot be holden of the tomb a single hour after it shall have begun to dawn towards the first day of the millennial week, because then their sentence will have terminated. This is the overcomer's hope,—the reward so much earlier, as well as more glorious, than we have dreamed of! the crown so much sooner, as well as brighter, than we have imagined! The devout Lavater, meditating on this point, exclaims: "How inexpressibly animating to the best exercise of our moral powers must this idea be,—to be a thousand years sooner in the enjoyment of the full fruition of the blessed! So much earlier—a thousand years earlier—to enjoy personal fellowship with the lovely Saviour and the noblest of the human family, and, along with Jesus, the prophets and apostles, to superintend the immediate concerns of the Godhead."

First in character also will be this pre-millennial resurrection; its preëminent glory being that upon those who attain to it "the second death hath no power." Here is the true harvest of which Christ is "the First-fruits." How can that Scripture be true which declares that Christ *is first born from the dead*" (Coloss. i. 19)? Had not several returned from death before Christ rose,—the Shunamite's son at the prayer of the prophet, and Lazarus and the widow's son at the call of Jesus? How, then, was He "*the first begotten of the dead*" (Rev. i. 5)? The answer seems obvious. These were raised to die again. Wondrous as was the transaction which restored them to life, it was only this mortal putting on mortality, and this corruptible putting on corruption. But "Christ being raised from the dead *dieth no more; death hath no more dominion over Him*" (Rom. vi. 6). The gospel of the resurrection which we preach, therefore, has no peer or rival in that which nature presents to us. Beautiful and oft-recurring as is the latter, it whispers no hint of immortality. Of a mortal resurrection which the Scriptures foretell for some, we see tokens and similitudes all about us in nature—in the flower springing up from the seed which has fallen into the earth and died; in the morning opening the vast grave of night, and summoning a sleeping world to rise and meet the sun "as he cometh forth as a bridegroom from his chamber;" in the springtide calling the earth from the tomb of winter, loosing her shroud of snow, and clothing her with renewed life and beauty: in all these there are joyful parables and pledges of a resurrection. But the flower fades and dies, the morning sinks again into the embrace of night, and the earth lies down once more in the sepulchre of winter; and so, alas! these symbols only mock the hope they have kindled in the soul. But while we are asking sorrowfully, "Is there no resurrection that is exempt from death?" this great text breaks upon our ears: "Blessed and holy is He that hath part in the first resurrection; *on such the second death hath no power.*" Christ's resurrection is the epitome of His Church's. As He rose only after a definite and divinely appointed time of resting in the grave, so will His people. That unseemly snatching for the crown of life which characterizes the latest improved eschatology—the theory that every man rises from the dead as soon as the breath is out of the body—has no foundation in Scripture.[73] Indeed, it has none in reason, unless we can admit that death is equivalent to life; elimination to resurrection; the falling down of this tabernacle of clay to its standing up. This is the revived error of Hymeneus and Philetus which makes the resurrection to be past already; it places our

---

[73] Professor Christlieb well says: "Whoever denies the bodily resurrection should be honest enough no longer to speak of resurrection at all. *Resurrection does not refer to the spirit*, the continued existence of which the Scripture takes as a matter of course, *but only to the body, and its issuing forth alive from the grave*. Only that can rise again which has been laid down in the grave, and that is only the body, not the spirit."—*Modern Doubt and Christian Belief*, p. 449.

hope in what is death's victory over us rather than our victory over death; it promises us a bodiless spirit in place of that "spiritual body" which is our redemption-birthright. "This immortal spirit shall put off its mortal coil" is the doctrine of philosophy; "This mortal shall put on immortality" is the doctrine of Scripture. Do we not see what transcendent honor is thus put upon the body in its promotion to incorruptibility? This in which we dwell—"the temple of the Holy Ghost"—is not our "vile body," as it is misleadingly called in the common version; though, because of the shadow of the curse which rests upon it, it is that in which "we groan being burdened." But itself shall be changed by the coming Lord, the very fabric and substance of it transformed and glorified. And because restoration rather than evolution is so distinctly taught in Scripture, we are certified of our continued physical identity, as it is written: "From whence also we wait for a Saviour, the Lord Jesus Christ, *who shall fashion anew the body of our humiliation, that it may be conformed to the body of His glory*" (Phil. iv. 21, R. V.). The charcoal and the diamond are the same substance; only that one is carbon in its humiliation, and the other carbon in its glory. So is this tabernacle in which we now dwell, in comparison with our house which is from heaven. The one is mortal flesh shadowed by the curse, and doomed to be "sown in dishonor;" the other is that flesh made immortal and marvelously transfigured. This house of clay, endeared to us by so many associations, is, therefore, only to be untenanted for a brief while, that we may move into it again wondrously refitted and beautified by its divine Fashioner. This thought, if cherished, may heal the homesickness which so often comes over us in the thought of death. For observe the exquisite balancing of those two household words—ἐνδημοῦντες and ἐκδημοῦντες —in Paul's Epistle to the Corinthians: "Knowing that while we are *at home* in the body, we are *from home* from the Lord, . . . and willing rather to be *from home* from the body, and *at home* with the Lord" (2 Cor. v. 6). But this home-dwelling with our Redeemer, as the connection shows, is not attained by our being unclothed, but clothed upon, with our house which is from heaven, that mortality may be swallowed up of life. It is when we become immortal residents in an immortal body that we are forever at home: "*So* shall we be ever with the Lord: wherefore comfort one another with these words." Having these promises, therefore, we should eagerly look upward, in patient waiting for our house from heaven, seeking the consummation of our hope, not in the putting off of this our tabernacle, but in the putting on of that. After his ardent prayer that he "might attain unto the resurrection from the dead," the apostle adds: "I press towards the mark for the prize of the up-calling"—τῆς ἄνω κλήσεως—"of God in Christ Jesus." Let who will fasten their hope upon the down-calling of mortality: "Return unto dust, ye children of men;" we will listen patiently and joyfully for the up-calling of immortality: "Awake and sing, ye that dwell in the dust, for thy dew is as the dew of herbs, and the earth shall cast out her dead" (Is. xxvi. 19).

V.
THE TRANSLATION OF THE CHURCH.

THE most startling; and except for the testimony of the "sure word of prophecy" the most incredible, transaction of which we can conceive, is that set forth in the words, "*caught up to meet the Lord in the air.*" The lightning-flash of the advent, dazzling and blinding for a moment; the swift transition of the cloud-chariot, and then "*forever with the Lord,*"—this is the brief description of the ecstatic scene which we call the Church's translation (1 Thess. iv. 15-18).

It is a twofold event, affecting the sainted dead and the saints that are living at the time of the *parousia*, and bringing both into one condition. "*The dead in Christ* shall rise first; then *we which are alive and remain* shall be caught up together with them." This order and distinction are revealed in several passages where the casual reader might not discover them. In the story of the raising of Lazarus—that enacted prophecy of the first resurrection—they are distinctly marked (John xi.). Beautiful miniature of the Church is that home in Bethany, whose crowning honor is this, that "Jesus loved Martha and her sister and Lazarus." Like the body of Christ to-day, a part living and a part dead,—"our friend Lazarus sleepeth,"—this household was waiting the coming of the Lord. But notwithstanding the sickness and dying that were ravaging that home, Jesus "*abode two days still in the same place where He was,*" just as He has already remained away from His Church nearly two millenniums—"one day is with the Lord as a thousand years, and a thousand years as one day"—while sickness and mourning and death have been holding sway. Then the advent announcement, for which we also wait, was heard, "Our friend Lazarus sleepeth; but *I go that I may awake him out of sleep.*" Such will be the blessed errand on which our Lord will come when the time of His return arrives. "Then Martha, as soon as she heard that Jesus was coming, *went and met Him*", even as the wise virgins will do when He shall come again; "but Mary sat still in the house," like those of the other company, the unwatchful and ungirded ones.

Then hear the Lord's great advent exposition: "I am the *Resurrection* and the *Life*: he that believeth in Me, *though he were dead, yet shall he live*, and whosoever *liveth and believeth in Me shall never die.*" It is no mere rhetorical amplification which we find here. This double office of Christ, and the corresponding twofold work, exactly match the declaration in the First Epistle to the Thessalonians (iv. 17). He is "the Resurrection" to those who shall be in their graves at the time of His coming; He is "the Life" to those who shall then be on the earth. To the first class He alludes when He says, "though he were dead, yet shall he live;" to the second He refers in the saying: "Whosoever liveth and believeth in Me shall never die." But both, in a moment, in the twinkling of an eye, shall be brought into the same condition of "glorified corporeity" at the sound of the last trumpet.[74]

Need we say that the transfiguration—that vivid tableau of the glorious appearing of our Lord—exhibits the same truth in unmistakable outline: "And, behold, there talked with Him two men, which were Moses and Elias, who appeared in glory." These two men were the representatives of the two classes just named. Moses, coming up from his unknown sepulchre in the valley of Moab, as the forerunner of the dead who shall be raised at the advent of Christ; and Elias, returning from the presence of the Lord, as the representative of those who taste not of death, but are translated,—these, standing together with the Lord in transfiguration glory on the Mount, present to us a radiant rehearsal, a glowing epitome, of the coming and kingdom of Jesus Christ.

If we turn to the great resurrection discourse of Paul in the fifteenth of 1 Corinthians, we find at the culmination of the argument the same double reference: "For the trumpet shall sound, and *the dead shall be raised incorruptible,* and *we shall be changed.*" Here are the two parties to the final transfiguration; and they are in an instant brought into the company of One for whom they both had been waiting.

Incomparably beautiful are the prophet's inspired words, when freed from the translator's interpolated words: "Thy dead shall live, *my dead body shall they arise*" (Isaiah xxvi. 19). The sainted sleepers, though under the deep humiliation of corruption, he disdains not still to call "my body." Strangers

---

[74] Let it be noticed that the second company named by Christ and the second company named by Paul are described by precisely the same form of speech, the timeless present participle: πᾶς ὁ ζῶν καὶ πιστεύων, "*all the living and believing*" (John xi. 25); ἡμεῖς οἱ ζῶντες οἱ περιλειπόμενοι, "*we the living, the remaining*" (1 Thess. iv. 17).

and pilgrims in the earth, they have pitched their tents in the grave for a night, saying with their Lord: "Moreover, *my flesh shall tabernacle in hope.*" And the first incident in the advent consummation will be the summons for these sojourners in the tomb to strike their tents, and, with the living, to take up their march to meet the coming Bridegroom in the air. "For this corruptible must put on incorruption, and this mortal must put on immortality." Here we must believe in no mere skillful balancing of inspired rhetoric, but a double designation to distinguish a double company,—those that are dead and those that are alive at the coming of Christ. For whether or not the first member of the sentence describes those whose flesh has seen corruption, the second member unquestionably applies to the living and their change: "So when this corruptible shall have put on incorruption, and this mortal shall have put on immortality, then shall be brought to pass the saying that is written, *Death is swallowed up in victory.*"[75] For then those upon the earth under sentence of death, and those in the earth under the dominion of death, will shout together their triumph over the last enemy.

As the daily watchers for the Lord's return, it is our dear hope that we may be in the company who shall not see death. This was the aspiration of Paul, expressed in the words: "Not for that we would be unclothed, but clothed upon, *that mortality might be swallowed up of life.*" He speaks not here of resurrection, but of transfiguration; not of death swallowed up in victory, but of the swifter and more immediate transition of mortality swallowed up of life. With the secret wherewith he comforted others—"Behold, I show you a mystery: we shall not all sleep, but we shall all be changed"—he now comforts himself, while groaning and burdened in this tabernacle. It is the most thrilling thought conceivable for those who are all their lifetime subject to bondage through fear of death, that, instead of being unclothed by the ghastly hands of death, they may be clothed upon by the transfiguring touch of life; that,

---

[75] Lange's *Commentary* criticises Bengel's view of this passage, that "the epithets 'corruptible' and 'mortal' (1 Cor. xv. 53) are to be distinguished as though the former applied to the dead and the latter to the living." But though the first word, φθαρτός,—*corruptible,*—may refer to the living, its cognate forms, employed in verses 42 and 52, apply to the dead. And we thence infer that "*this corruptible*" designates the same class. "*This mortal,*"—θνητός—on the contrary, is defined in the Thayer-Grimm Greek Lexicon to mean "*subject to death, and so still living*" (cf. Rom. vi. 12; viii. 2; 2 Cor. iv. 2; v. 4). We think Bengel's view is reasonable, and not fanciful.

instead of the winding-sheet of the grave, there may be the immediate enswathement of the garments of glory. But to whichever company we may belong, the shout of triumph will be ours: "O Death, where is thy sting? O Grave, where is thy victory?"

Reunion with the descending Saviour is the first experience in the great transaction. "Caught up *to meet the Lord* in the air,"—these words are crowded with suggestion, since they always signify to meet and return with. As the disciples in Rome went out to meet Paul when they heard of his approach, and accompanied him to the city; as the wise virgins are pictured as going forth to meet the bridegroom and attending him to the house of the bride,—so by the same form of speech it is here implied that the Church will be raptured away to join the Lord on His advancing way, and escort Him back to the earth.[76] It is not true, as some have judged from this passage, either that the Lord comes no further than the upper air, or that believers depart forever from this lower world. This is rather the Redeemer's royal return to the earth. We remember how, on the visit of a great general to our city,—after he had conquered peace and saved the country,—a delegation of our most honored citizens went out a few miles beyond the borders of the town to welcome and conduct him to the metropolis. Thus will God's elect, the transfigured Bride of Christ, go forth at the sound of the trumpet to meet the Bridegroom upon the suburbs of our globe, to attend Him earthward.

Triumphal entry, indeed! Earth, that once rejected her Lord, and sent Him back alone to heaven with five wounds upon His person, will furnish a majestic convoy for His return. "The glorious company of the apostles, the noble army of martyrs, the Holy Church throughout all the world,"—these, whom the world knew not, even as it knew Him not, now raised and transfigured, will constitute an innumerable white-robed retinue to attend Him onward as He comes at last to accomplish the restitution of all things. And yet, so far as we can read the outlines of prophecy, we infer that there will be a pause in the march of this descending procession,—how long we do not conjecture,—while the advent judgments are visited upon Christendom. For

---

[76] Acts xxviii. 15; Matt. xxv. 6. The phrase of our text—εἰς ἀπάντησιν—is used in both these other instances, and nowhere else in the New Testament. The circumstances in each case define its meaning, showing it to signify, as Alford says, "*meeting one who is approaching*, not merely meeting with a person."

observe in the prophet Isaiah that, following the summons of the dead, "Awake and sing, ye that dwell in the dust," there is the gracious call: "*Come, my people, enter thou into thy chambers, and shut thy doors about thee; hide thyself, as it were, for a little moment, until the indignation be overpast. For, behold, the Lord cometh out of His place to punish the inhabitants of the earth for their iniquity: the earth also shall disclose her blood, and shall no more cover her slain*" (Isaiah xxvi. 20, 21). As Noah was hidden in the ark when the judgment of the flood came upon the earth; as the disciples, being forewarned by Christ, were sheltered in the hill-top of Pella, beyond Jordan, during the bloody siege in which Jerusalem perished,—so shall it be with those who are accounted worthy to escape the judgments poured out upon apostate Christendom. They shall be wrapped away in a sheltering pavilion of cloud, and hidden in some angel-guarded retreat on high, where the apostle's word shall be fulfilled to them: "And to you who are troubled, *rest with us*, when the Lord Jesus shall be revealed from heaven, with His mighty angels, in flaming fire, taking vengeance on them that know not God and obey not the gospel of our Lord Jesus Christ" (2 Thess. i. 7, 8).

As to the deep questions of when? and how? connected with this transporting theme, we must not speak dogmatically. We get suggestive hints, however, from type and parallel, as well as from literal prophecy. "*Enoch, the seventh from Adam*, prophesied of these, saying, Behold, the Lord cometh with ten thousand of His saints" (Jude 14). He not only prophesied, but was himself a prophecy,—a literal prototype of those who shall be translated and not see death. As he was the "seventh from Adam," these raptured ones, we expect, will belong to the seventh millennium from creation; and as the history of his change is condensed into these brief words, "*And he was not, for God took him*," so will theirs be. Unheralded and unnoted by the great busy world, so far as we can judge, will be this transaction. "Behold, I come as a thief!" says our Lord. Not one of the sleeping household saw the midnight robber as he crept in and snatched the jewels, and silently stole away. "And they shall be mine, saith the Lord of hosts, *in that day when I make up my jewels*" (Mal. iii. 17). But the world will not know its loss until they are gone, the wheat gathered in and the tares left; the jewels snatched away and the casket remaining. Then, at last, will they "discern between the righteous and the wicked, between him that serveth God and him that serveth Him not," as the day has now come that burns as an oven, "in which all that do wickedly shall be stubble," and the Lord sits "as a refiner and purifier of silver." True, it is written that "the trumpet shall sound" at the ushering in of this great transaction; but as the outer world has not heard the Apocalyptic trumpets as they have successively sounded, they may not hear "the sound of the last trump." True, it is said also, that "the Lord Himself shall descend from heaven with a shout;" but this κέλευσμα, or summons, may be only for the ears of the faithful, who, like a retreating army, shall now be silently withdrawn from a judgment-doomed Christendom.

And yet, upon this whole question of a secret rapture, we would speak with reserve, knowing that there are scriptures which give a different impression. But the event itself, hidden or manifest, is a most inspiring one in the influence which it carries. "The translation of Enoch," says Dr. Owen, "is a divine testimony that *the body itself is capable of eternal life.*" And this transaction, like Peter's vision, has been thrice repeated,—in the Patriarchal age by Enoch; in the Prophetic age by Elijah; and in the Gospel age by Christ,—that we might not forget the lesson which it teaches.[77] With such a vision before our eyes, we should cease talking of the immortality of the soul, as though we knew not that God had provided some better thing for us. It is a lamentable apostasy from Paulism to Platonism to substitute the hope of being "unclothed" for that of being "clothed upon."

Let philosophers dream of a naked immortality as man's highest estate in the life to come, but we will be content with nothing less than God's full provision of this mortal putting on immortality. Therefore the conception of the body as the spirit's clog and prison-house should find no place in a Christian eschatology. It may, indeed, sometimes be so in our present fallen and disordered condition. But the transfiguration will forever abolish such an anomaly, giving us a winged body in the place of a weighted spirit. If heathen moralism spoke the best it knew in the famous saying of Plotinus, that "he was

---

[77] "Not infrequently we substitute for the fullness of the Christian creed the purely philosophical conception of an immortality of the soul, which destroys, as we shall see hereafter, the idea of the continuance of our distinct personal existence. Nothing is more common than to hear it assumed that the *soul* is the whole self. Yet nothing can be more clear upon reflection than that the only self of which we are conscious is made up of *soul* and *body*."—Westcott, *Gospel of the Resurrection*, pp. 6, 138.

thankful he was not *tied to an immortal body*," let not Christianity fail to speak the best it knows in the rejoicing of its disciples that they shall be untied, indeed, from this mortal, but only to be *translated in an immortal body*. "They shall mount up with wings as eagles; they shall run and not be weary; they shall walk and not faint."

VI.
THE MARRIAGE OF THE LAMB.

THE bridal relationship of the Church to her Lord is so profound an idea that we are not surprised to find its roots deeply embedded in the history and prophecy and poetry of the Old Testament. Not to dwell upon the typical fore-shadowings of this truth contained in the story of Abraham's servant seeking a bride for Isaac, and of Jacob's seven years' service for Rachel; and not to enlarge upon the gracious words of Jehovah to His people, "I will betroth them unto Me forever; and as the bridegroom rejoiceth over the bride, so shall thy God rejoice over thee,"—we find in the Canticles the most complete and vivid setting forth of this conception. The central idea of the Song of Solomon is the same as that of the Apocalypse. According to Ewald, the commentator, who has given the most subtle analysis of this exquisite poem, the plot is this: "On the one hand, a king in all the splendors of his glory, transported with admiration, overflowing with passion; on the other, the poor and simple shepherd to whom the Shulamite has plighted her faith; the former present, the latter absent; *the maiden called to decide freely between these two rivals.* Such is the conflict in all its moral grandeur."

Translating Oriental poetry into Apocalyptic symbolism, the Book of Revelation yields us the same conception.[78] Immanuel, the Shepherd Bridegroom, feeding His flock in Paradise, is ever sending word to His espoused Church on earth, "Behold, I come quickly." But she, in her long waiting, is constantly solicited and wooed by royal suitors—purple and gold and precious stones being offered her—to withdraw her heart from her heavenly Consort, and to accept a throne with the kings of the earth. The harlot bride, a fallen daughter of God, clothed with scarlet and decked with jewels, and living in fornication with the rulers of this world, appears upon the scene, hating and hunting this unsullied spouse of Christ and driving her into exile. But in spite

---

[78]   "The Seer
That, ere he died, saw all the grievous times
Of the fair Bride—who with the lance and nails
Was won,"—Dante.

of all these trials of her faith on the one hand, and all these solicitations of kings and these proffers of Solomonic wealth and splendor on the other, her heart is still true to her absent Lord, and her noble answer is, "Many waters cannot quench love, neither can the floods drown it; *if a man would give all the substance of his house for love it would be utterly contemned*" (Cant. viii. 7).

And yet the trial is one of intense and protracted severity. Her Lord delays His return long beyond her expectation; and the world mocks at her bridal hope, incredulously asking, "Where is the sign of His coming?" Beside, it is an invisible and far-off Lover to whom her heart is plighted, one who appears only in visions of hope, and "who in His sublime austerity scorns to use any sensuous means for attracting His people to Himself." In a word, her choice must be between an earthly Solomon, crowned with present glory and honor, and the Beloved whom the world has rejected, and who now stands without, knocking, His head wet with the dews of the night. "Sometimes He comes down and manifests Himself to the eyes of her faith. She sees Him as in a dream; she delights herself spiritually with His presence,—then suddenly He vanishes. And then once more she is alone, carrying on the contest with Solomon, who draws near in all his pomp, and tries to cast his spell upon her. But she remains faithful to Him who is invisible; she sees the moment approaching in which, the true love of her God having won the victory in her heart over all the arts of the seducer, she will be fetched away by Him, and—more fortunate in this respect than the Shulamite herself—will be able to follow Him to those spiced mountains where He pastures His flock amongst the lilies."[79]

That moment has now come; the Bridegroom appears in the clouds of heaven to take His betrothed one to Himself; and this is "the marriage of the Lamb."

For mark the significant fact, that the Church is only *affianced* to Christ as yet, not married. "*I have espoused you to one husband that I may present you as a chaste virgin to Christ,*" writes Paul to the Corinthians, speaking by the Holy Ghost. All through the time of His absence "the Spirit and *the Bride say, Come.*" But not until He appears in glory, and translates the Church, does the Bride become the wife: "Come hither and I will show thee the Bride, *the Lamb's wife.*" The convent language, therefore, in which the veiled nun is

---

[79] Godet, *Studies on the Old Testament*, p. 329.

declared to be "wedded to Christ," is entirely foreign to the teaching of Scripture. For these holy nuptials are not with the individual, but with the whole Church, and therefore they cannot be consummated till all the faithful—the quick and the dead—are brought into one company. As long as the Saviour is still absent from His people, it is the Church's fast-day, not her feast-day. "Can the children of the bride-chamber fast while the Bridegroom is with them? As long as they have the Bridegroom with them they cannot fast. *But the days will come when the Bridegroom shall be taken away from them; then shall they fast, in those days*" (Mark ii. 19, 20). This describes the present attitude of the Church,—one of patient waiting and chastened sobriety "till He come." As often as she breaks the bread and drinks the cup, she may say to her Lord: "*Thou preparest a table before me in the presence of mine enemies.*" But not yet are His words fulfilled to her: "*That ye may eat and drink at My table, in My kingdom.*" All attempts at premature wedlock with Christ, by making the communion a feast of His "real presence," instead of a fast for His real absence, does violence to that virgin-instinct of the Church which knows that there can be no true nuptials until the Bridegroom comes, as there can be no real reign of the saints until the King appears.

For where is the true Bride of Christ at this time? Before the face of her enemy she has "fled *into the wilderness*, where she hath a place prepared of God, that they should feed her there, a thousand two hundred and threescore days" (Rev. xii. 6). The time of the Harlot's enthronement is the time of the Bride's exile; while the one is sharing a crown with the princes of this world, who crucified the Lord of glory, the other is sharing rejection with Him whom the world knew not. What pathetic sorrows are hers during all this wilderness period! Because she will not be seduced from her bridal affection, all manner of opprobrium is heaped upon her. Even the watchmen, when they find her, smite her and wound her, and the keepers of the walls take away her veil from her. But in spite of all violence and scorn of men, her heart is with the absent Bridegroom, saying: "I charge you, O daughters of Jerusalem, if ye find my Beloved, that ye tell Him that I am sick of love."

> "My heart is with Him on the throne,
> And ill can brook delay;
> Each moment listening for His voice:
> 'Rise up and come away.'"

But now the long hoped-for consummation has arrived. The cry, "Behold, the Bridegroom cometh, go ye out to meet Him," sounds upon the air. She who kept her garments unspotted from the world is ready to be married, and stands clothed in her wedding vesture: she, also, who lived wantonly with the kings of the earth, is ready to be condemned, and stands "arrayed in purple and scarlet color, and decked with gold and precious stones." Hardly has the "*Alleluia*" over the judgment of "the great Harlot which did corrupt the earth with her fornication" died away, before another is heard: "*Alleluia*, for the Lord God omnipotent reigneth. Let us be glad, and rejoice, and give honor to Him: for the marriage of the Lamb is come, and His wife hath made herself ready" (Rev. xix. 6, 7). It is the hour of blissful fruition for the waiting Bride: "*Who is this that cometh up from the wilderness leaning upon her beloved?*" (Cant. viii. 5.) Who, indeed, but she whose countenance was often bedewed with tears, whose feet were often torn with the thorns of the desert through which her enemies pursued her? But now the reproach of her widowhood is taken away, the bridal veil is upon her face, and the nuptial joy is in her heart.

The end of the Redeemer's spousal love is at last made manifest: "Husbands, love your wives, even as Christ also loved the Church and gave Himself for it," writes the apostle. And to what purpose was this divine affection? "That He might sanctify and cleanse it with the washing of water by the word;" this is what he is now accomplishing by the ministry of the Holy Spirit. "That He might present it to Himself, a glorious Church, not having spot, or wrinkle, or any such thing, but that it should be holy and without blemish" (Eph. v. 25-27): this is what He is yet to accomplish by the ministry of His second coming. How striking the language! Himself to Himself,"— αὐτὸς ἑαυτῷ,—"Christ permits neither attendants nor paranymphs to present the Bride; He alone presents, He receives."[80] And He gives her to Himself in completed sanctification and transfigured beauty. St. Paul was jealous over the Corinthian Christians, that he "might present them as a chaste virgin to Christ." But Immanuel receives this virgin not only as chaste, but as chastened; not only as sanctified through trial, but as at last glorified through rapture. Often she may have been tempted to murmur at the hardship of her lot, and the severity of her wilderness portion. But all this is not worthy to be

---

[80] Ellicott.

compared with the glory that is now revealed in her as she stands at the Bridegroom's side, and hears Him saying to her: "I remember for thee the kindness of thy youth, the love of thine espousal, when thou wentest after me in the wilderness, in a land that is not sown" (Jer. ii. 2, R. V.).

And there is not only a presentation, but a manifestation, in which obscurity and obloquy give place to glory and honor.

It has happened within our knowledge that a wealthy and cultivated gentleman became affianced to a maiden of the lowest and poorest condition. Because he had set his love upon her, he took her out of her poverty and ignorance, and sent her to a distant school to be educated and fitted for her appointed sphere. After years of discipline and preparation, he withdrew her from her retreat and brought her to his home, where a splendid reception was given her, and she was publicly introduced into the society in which she was henceforth to move as his wife. Precisely thus has Christ dealt with His Church,—sending her into long wilderness discipline to be trained for her heavenly associations. But now that the time of her humiliation is ended, He brings her forth to receive her visible manifestation and royal dowry. Whereas she has "esteemed the reproach of Christ as greater riches than the treasures of Egypt," now is manifested in her "what is the riches of the glory of His inheritance in the saints;" and whereas she has been counted "the offscouring of all things" for His sake, she is now exalted before the eyes of men and angels with Him who has come "to be glorified in His saints, and to be admired in all them that believe." In a word, the Bride who has shared her Lord's rejection now shares His throne as the wife of the Lamb, the Queen-consort of the King of kings. Here is the crowning joy of the redeemed. He and His are no more twain; but one; the "little while" of their separation is at last swallowed up in the "forever with the Lord." They see His face; His name is in their foreheads; they hear His voice: "Eat, O friends: drink, yea, drink abundantly, O beloved." "Blessed are they which are called unto the marriage supper of the Lamb."

VII.
THE JUDGMENT OF CHRISTENDOM.

THE first resurrection and the rapture of the saints have carried our contemplation heavenward; but it is now recalled to what is passing on the earth. The one transaction is the exact reverse of the other. The Virgin Bride is called upward to the marriage supper of the Lamb; the apostate Spouse of Christ is now cast down and publicly divorced by her long dishonored Lord. The punishment meted out to her—"These shall hate the harlot, and shall make her desolate and naked, and shall eat her flesh and *burn her with fire*" (Rev. xvii. 16)—is according to a very ancient law: "And the daughter of any priest, if she profane herself by playing the whore, she profaneth her father: *she shall be burnt with fire*" (Lev. xxi. 9). This fallen daughter of God has persisted in her fornication with the kings of the earth for centuries; and they with whom she has glorified herself and lived deliciously now turn against her and become the providential instruments of her destruction, saying to the Almighty: "Thy daughter-in-law hath played the harlot: bring her forth and let her be burnt" (Gen. xxxviii. 24). Graphic and lifelike to the highest degree are the delineations of the papal apostasy. As the true Church of Christ is set forth under the double similitude of a bride and of a city, so is the false. And one has only closely to compare the details of the harlot's photograph in Rev. xvii. with the lurid painting of Babylon the Great in Rev. xviii. to perceive that the subject is the same in each. The scarlet and purple, the gold and precious stones and pearls, are found in both descriptions: the same sin of wantonness with the kings of the earth; the same indictment of persecuting God's saints; and the same doom of being "utterly burned with fire" belong to each. Only in the first portrayal the kings of the earth are seen executing the divine vengeance upon the apostate bride; while in the second they are represented as bewailing and lamenting her doom, even as a profligate will sometimes weep and mourn over his murdered paramour.

This judgment seems to be executed in two stages, gradual and sudden, harmonizing with the two stages of the judgment of the Man of Sin as foretold in Thessalonians: "Whom the Lord shall *consume* with the breath of His mouth, and *destroy* with the brightness of His coming."

The first process is described thus: "*And the ten horns which thou sawest and the beast, these shall hate the harlot, and shall make her desolate and naked, and shall eat her flesh, and shall burn her with fire*" (Rev. xvii. 16). The beast here must be the same which carries the harlot; it cannot be an individual Antichrist, therefore, else we should have the grotesque figure of the woman riding upon a man, a symbolical monstrosity of which revelation could not be guilty. Besides, there is no precedent in Scripture for making a beast signify an individual man. If Daniel gives the key to Revelation, as is generally admitted, a beast means a dynasty or civil government. It is the *body* of the beast, the Papal Empire, with its ten kingdoms, including rulers, people, territory, and dominion, that is here evidently meant. These that have long supported the harlot church now turn and rend her. It is useless to say that by identifying the papacy with the beast, this verse would compel the conclusion that the Roman Pope finally destroys the Roman Church. There is a *Head* and a *Body* of the true Church; the Head is called *The Christ*, ὁ Χριστός (1 Cor. xi. 13), and the Body is called *The Christ*, ὁ Χριστός (1 Cor. xii. 12); but it does not follow, therefore, that when it is said that "Christ loved the Church and gave Himself for it," we must conclude that He loved Himself and gave Himself for Himself; for though Christ and the Church are mystically one, their actions and offices are separable. So the papacy, as *head* of the Roman Empire in its ten-kingdomed condition, is called the beast (Rev. xiii. 4, 5, 6); and the empire itself, as the body, is called the beast (Rev. xvii. 3). But though symbolically one, their actions and career are distinguishable. It is clearly the body of the beast that is figured as carrying and supporting the harlot,—the Roman Empire under the sway of the Roman Church, the empire supporting the Church, and the Church ruling the empire. But when the consuming judgments begin, this is changed. Just what was predicted, we have lived to see,—the kingdoms once subject to the papacy snapping their concordats and alliances, till the woman's bit and bridle are utterly broken; those kingdoms turning upon her and stripping her of her endowments, rejecting her authority, and tearing away her territory. So we have beheld it wonderfully come to pass in these latter days. Events often constitute an indisputable exegesis. So long ago as A. D. 1607, Brightman, the commentator, "searching what and what manner of time" the Spirit signified by this prophecy, concluded that about A. D. 1800 the dismantlement of the Roman Church would begin. In August, 1797, the French ambassador in Rome wrote to Napoleon: "Discontent is at its height in the papal states; the government will fall to pieces of itself. We are making it *consume by a slow fire.* It will soon crumble into dust." The next year the papal government was overthrown, and an infidel democracy reared on its ruins. "The churches and convents," says Alison, "the palaces of the cardinals and nobility, were laid waste. The spoliation exceeded all that the Goths and Vandals had effected."[81] A further exhibition of the same process of consumption we have witnessed, especially in Italy and in France, since the recent loss of the pope's temporal power.

Then follows a subsequent stage in the retribution, when the awful cry breaks upon our ears: *"Fallen, fallen is Babylon the Great!"* It is history repeating itself. Every age has ended in judgment, and so shall the present dispensation close. As apostate Judaism met its doom in the destruction of Jerusalem; so apostate Christendom expiates its sentence in the overthrow of mystical Babylon. This destruction will fall, we believe, upon the literal city of seven hills, as the visible centre and capital of the apostasy. What other systems beside the papal may be involved in the judgment is a most solemn question to be pondered. It is plainly intimated that the mother has daughters, and therefore that Babylon the Great has outlying suburbs which are in fellowship with her. Let him that readeth understand. The extent of this judgment needs to be carefully considered, since some would discredit the plain interpretation which we follow, by declaring that it implies the consigning of every subject of the pope to perdition, as it is declared that "if any man worship the beast and his image, and receive his mark in his forehead or in his hand," he shall be consigned to everlasting punishment. But here the analogy of previous judgments throws striking light. Before the doom of fire and brimstone fell upon Sodom, the warning was sounded,—"Up! get thee out of this place, for the Lord will destroy this city;" and heeding the call, some were found sheltered in little Zoar ere the burning rain descended. So, likewise, before Jerusalem was destroyed, the Saviour's previous admonition was enforced: "Then let them which be in Judea flee to the mountains;" and the holy seed gained refuge from the awful slaughter in the hilltop of Pella.

---

[81] *Closing Days of Christendom*, Wale, p. 362.

The Apocalypse predicts a similar warning before the fall of Babylon: "Come out of her, my people, that ye be not partakers of her sins." This summons, we believe, is synchronous, or nearly so, with the descending of the Lord in glory (Rev. xviii. 4). We conclude this because the Church is summoned to exercise judgment,—"*Reward her even as she rewarded you, and double unto her according to her works*"—which she is everywhere forbidden to do in her present suffering state, but which she is to do at the time of her reign and judgment with Christ at His coming in glory. Before the sentence goes forth, "Babylon the Great is fallen," the gracious call of separation will have been sounded: "*Come forth, my people, out of her,*" and then "they that are Christ's at His coming," whether hitherto in Babylon or without her, whether in their graves or living on the earth, will be caught up to meet the Lord in the air, where, standing with the Lamb upon Mount Zion with the hundred and forty-four thousand having the Father's name written in their foreheads, they shall see afar off the doom of such as persisted in worshiping the beast and wearing his name upon their brows. As some true saints of God have been found in Rome during all her history, so we doubt not it will be to the end. But overwhelming doom will fall upon such as persevere in their idolatries after this last warning cry shall have been sounded. If *then* "any man is worshiping the beast, and receiving his mark on his forehead or upon his hand," "the same shall drink of the wine of the wrath of God, which is poured out without mixture into the cup of his indignation"[82] (Rev. xiv. 9).

Hark the song of exultation breaking forth from heaven! A great voice of much people—of myriads whose blood the harlot drank—is now heard saying: "Alleluia! salvation, and glory, and honor, and power unto the Lord

---

[82] "Covetous Babylon of wrath divine,
    By its worst crimes, has drained the full cup now.
    * * *
    Her idols shall be shattered in the dust,
    Her proud towers, enemies of heaven, be hurled,
    Her wardens into flames and exile thrust.
    Fair souls and friends of virtue shall the world
    Possess in peace; and we shall see it made
    All gold, and fully its old works displayed."
                  Petrarch, 1304-1374.

our God. For true and righteous are His judgments; for He hath judged the great whore which did corrupt the earth with her fornication, and hath avenged the blood of His servants at her hand" (Rev. xix. 2). And immediately a triumphal procession is seen moving forth from the direction whence comes the song: "And I saw heaven opened, and behold a white horse; and He that sat upon him was called Faithful and True, and in righteousness doth He judge and make war" (Rev. xix. 11). This majestic rider we met at the very opening of Apocalyptic history (vi. 2), but then He was going forth in peaceful conquest: "And I saw, and behold a white horse, and He that sat upon him had a bow,"—"*Thou didst ride upon thine horses, upon thy chariots of salvation: thy bow was made quite bare*" (Hab. iii. 9), "and *a crown was given unto Him.*" This is the "*stephanos*" the crown which in Scripture is so repeatedly set before the Christian as the prize for his spiritual overcoming, and which is fitly worn by Him who in the days of His flesh could say, "I have overcome the world." "And He went forth conquering and *in order to conquer,*"—not only to effect the present victories of redemption, but to win the ultimate sovereignty of the world.

This final conquest has now arrived; for as the white-horse rider comes forth from heaven, we behold, "and on His head were many crowns." Not the *stephanos* now, but the *diadema* is the symbol of His supremacy. The kingdom of the world has become the kingdom of our Lord and of his Christ; and all the crowns of all the kings have passed over upon His brow. The long succession of world-wide monarchies which we beheld in Daniel's vision has intervened; the stone cut out of the mountain without hands now smites the image upon its feet, and itself fills the whole world. How striking the picture of the final transfer of earth's sovereignty to Immanuel! To Nebuchadnezzar, king of Babylon, the first in this line of universal monarchs, God said: "Thou, O king, art *a king of kings*" (Dan. ii. 37). Now that this bloody line terminates in the overthrow of mystical Babylon—whose sovereign, the pope, has long arrogated both temporal and ecclesiastical supremacy—Messiah takes up both the successions and also takes the long abused title attaching thereto: "And He hath on His vesture and on His thigh a name written, *King of kings and Lord of lords*" (Rev. xix. 16).

It is necessary here to explain how this judgment of Christendom is related to that of the world as a whole. This will only be possible by giving careful attention to the law of prophetic perspective which rules so constantly in the divine predictions. That wondrous judgment parable of our Lord, recorded in the twenty-fifth of Matthew, seems to be opened out by later revelations so as to have an age-long reach. Resurrection and judgment are counterparts; and as the rising of the dead, foretold by Christ in the Gospel of John (v. 28), though seeming to be a simultaneous event for the righteous and for the wicked,—"The hour is coming in the which all that are in the graves shall hear His voice and shall come forth: they that have done good, unto the resurrection of life; and they that have done evil, unto the resurrection of damnation"—is shown in the later Revelation of John to take place in two stages a thousand years apart: so the judgments in which these respective resurrections issue are separated by an entire millennium Laying the prophecy of the xxvth of Matthew alongside this of the vth of John, we judge that they exactly harmonize; that the time when the Son of man shall "sit upon the throne of His glory" is the whole millennial period; that the time when the righteous dead shall hear the King say unto them, "Come, ye blessed of my Father, inherit the kingdom prepared for you from the foundation of the world," is at the coming of Christ in the beginning of the millennium, which is "the resurrection of life:" that time when the unrighteous dead shall hear the sentence, "Depart from me, ye cursed, into eternal fire," is at the close of the millennium, which is "the resurrection of condemnation." While this is so, we should not err in saying that in one sense the judgment of the righteous and of the wicked is simultaneous. For since resurrection is the great declarative act of justification, the coming forth of the righteous from the tomb at the advent of Christ is their open acquittal and vindication before the universe; while the non-resurrection of the wicked is their silent condemnation,—which silent condemnation, however, is to be made public and visible at the second resurrection and the great white-throne judgment at the end of the millennium.

It has been maintained that the scene in the xxvth of Matthew is strictly and only a judgment of the living nations. It is clearly this; but the question is, whether this prophetic picture of our Lord is not a composite photograph comprehending in a single view all the stages and subjects of the judgment.

While acknowledging the exceeding difficulty of harmonizing all the texts relating to this subject, we conceive of the great transaction thus: Judgment begins at the house of God when the Master of the house returns in the clouds of heaven. Instantly there is a separation of the wheat from the tares; of the sheep from the goats; of the Bride from the harlot. By resurrection and translation, the faithful living and the faithful dead are instantly brought into one company in the skies; by non-resurrection and devastating judgments, the apostate dead and the apostate living are brought into the other company in Hades. Thus, in a moment, in the twinkling of an eye, judgment is pronounced for both classes.

Now the reward of the righteous begins. That manifestation predicted in the words, "For we must all appear before the judgment-seat of Christ, that every one may receive the things done in his body according to that which he hath done, whether it be good or bad," at last takes place. This is not a judgment of believers as to the question of life or death; into such judgment it is distinctly declared they do not enter: "Verily, verily, I say unto you, he that heareth My word, and believeth on Him that sent Me, hath everlasting life, and shall not come into condemnation,"—κρίσιν, *judgment*—"but is passed from death unto life" (John v. 24). The first resurrection is itself the award of life; and they who now stand in their risen and immortal bodies have passed beyond all possible inquisition concerning the inheritance of life eternal. But into strict and solemn investigation concerning their works they do now come; for at length is that Scripture fulfilled: "Every man's work shall be made manifest; for the day shall declare it, because it shall be revealed by fire; and the fire shall try every man's work of what sort it is" (1 Cor. iii. 13). Doubtless there will stand before the Lord in that day many who are saved but unrewarded, redeemed by the precious blood of Christ, but not recompensed at the resurrection of the just; their works burned up as worthless, but themselves saved so as by fire (1 Cor. iii. 15). But to such as have borne the cross and endured hardness, this is the time of reward: "Behold, I come quickly and my reward is with me *to give to every man according as his work shall be.*" And this recompense we believe will consist in no vague and transcendental joys of song, and rapture, and repose. That repeated strain in the parable which follows that of the ten virgins—"Well done, good and faithful servant: thou hast been faithful over a few things, *I will make thee ruler over many things*"—seems to indicate the nature of the saints' inheritance. Reigning with Christ over the earth throughout the millennium, their rank in His manifested kingdom will be according to their fidelity during the time of His absence. In the judgment of the nations which now follows, they will be associated with their Lord,—"Know ye not that the saints shall judge the world?" (1 Cor. vi. 2)—and in their nearness to Him in honor and authority will consist the greatness of their reward. It is not necessary to believe that the saints' reward will be altogether earthly or civil, but nevertheless there is a meaning which must not be spiritualized away in the beatitude of our Lord: "Blessed are the meek, *for they shall inherit the earth*" (Matt. v. 5); and in the award of the nobleman returning from a far country to set up his kingdom: "Well, thou good servant: because thou hast been faithful in a very little, *have thou authority over ten cities*" (Luke xix. 17).

At the end of the millennium occurs the second resurrection. So far as there is a quickening of "the rest of the dead"—those left behind at the sound of the advent trumpet a thousand years before—it is strictly a "resurrection unto judgment." Here, in the vision of the great white throne which follows, we find "the book of life" opened, and "whosoever was not found written in the book of life was cast into the lake of fire." Those whose names *were* in the book have already been living and reigning with Christ a thousand years; therefore, unless we think of them as now leaving their thrones and crowns, and coming before the bar of God to be tried for their lives, we cannot conceive of their being the subjects of this solemn inquisition: and as we have already seen, the Scripture declares that they will not be, since they have already passed from death unto life, and come not into judgment.

But, holding that the righteous and unrighteous still die during the millennium, it appears that there will be saints as well as sinners in the second resurrection. Hence there will be for such a judgment of works when the assize of the great white throne and of Him that sits on it shall open. How solemnly, therefore, it reads: "And the sea gave up the dead which were in it; and death and hell delivered up the dead which were in them, and they were judged every man according to their works!" (Rev. xxi. 13.)

Such seems to be the order as we gaze through the long and solemn perspective of the judgment scene; but if our readers shall put a question-mark against many of our conclusions, we shall not be surprised. There is a massing of shadows and a concentration of mystery about the whole scene which invest it with unutterable awe. We are willing to leave the shadows unlifted and the mystery unsolved, if, "knowing therefore the terror of the Lord," we may "persuade men."

VIII.
THE RESTORATION OF ISRAEL.

THERE is a fragment of Jewish legend that has floated down to us, which represents two venerable rabbis as musing among the ruins of Jerusalem after its destruction. One is giving way to unrestrained lamentation, saying: "Alas! alas! this is the end of all. Our beautiful city is no more, our Temple is laid waste, our brethren are driven away into captivity." The other, with greater cheerfulness, replies: "True; but let us learn from the verity of God's judgments, which we behold about us, the certainty of His mercies. He hath said, 'I will destroy Jerusalem,' and we see that He hath done it. But hath He not also said, 'I will rebuild Jerusalem,' and shall we not believe Him?"

This is a correct method of reasoning, and one which we would commend to Gentile doctors as well as to Hebrew rabbis. A literal fulfillment of threatenings upon Israel argues a literal fulfillment of promises. The sorrowful and ill-starred history of the Jewish race since the dispersion has been the theme of constant reflection among thoughtful men. It is not merely the fact of their unparalleled sufferings which has arrested attention, but the evidence of a providential method, if we may say so, running through those sufferings, the appearance of their history having been woven at every point to the pattern of some hidden decree. Persecution which would have blotted out any other nation seems in their case to have been so blended and tempered with divine preservatives, that, like that symbol of their Jehovah, the burning bush, they present the astonishing spectacle of a nation always girdled about with the fires of judgment, but never consumed. Scattered like dust to the four winds, they have yet preserved their national unity as firm and compact as a rock; driven out of their land, and kept from it by an inexorable decree, they have beheld their supplanters guarding with scrupulous care their most sacred shrines, as though unconsciously waiting to surrender them back to them on the expiration of their lease; so utterly homeless that they have had no city or foot of land for centuries which they could call their own, they have, nevertheless, been the bankers of the world, as though destined always to have on deposit the wealth needful for restoring the desolations of Zion, if the hour for such restoration were to come. This mingling of mercy and misfortune in their career has constituted the Jewish race the paradox and miracle of modern history. It has awakened a constant curiosity and speculation in the minds of the thoughtful as to their future. Incomparably dark as has been their history for eighteen hundred years, men have been constrained to see in that darkness the shadow of Jehovah's hand turned over them for their protection and preservation! And in the very sharpness of the judgments that have overtaken them, not a few have discerned the presage of a future glory far surpassing anything in the past.

Have we thought what an undertone of hope there is even in the divine condemnations of the Jews? The single word "*until*" constitutes a kind of epitomized prophecy of Israel's restoration. The picture which our Lord gives in the gospels of the destruction of the Holy City and the dispersion of the Jews is one of the darkest in all Scripture. What a massing of the shadows of doom; what a crowding together of successive chapters of woe! And yet, as we reach the middle of that sentence which summarizes whole centuries of divine retribution, "Jerusalem shall be trodden of the Gentiles *until* the times of the Gentiles be fulfilled," we are conscious of a certain powerful relief from the strain that has been put upon us. "*Until*"—amid the dense surrounding darkness, this one word fairly gleams with the promise of a better future for the suffering race. It is only a hint, an intimation, that is given us; but it is so pregnant with the hidden light of hope, that it impels us instinctively to fix an end to the desolations of Zion. So in our Lord's pathetic farewell to the Temple, after His rejection, there is the same refrain, "Behold, your house is left unto you desolate;" and, "Verily I say unto you, Ye shall not see Me, until the time come when ye shall say, Blessed is He that cometh in the name of the Lord." *Until the time come,*—here, certainly, is a flash of light upon the dark prediction of Israel's desertion. It is but a word, again; but it is heavy with the burden of prophetic expectation. Next to the silence which says nothing contrary to our hope, the hint which barely breaks the silence in its favor is the most significant. And this is all we have here; but how much is in it! In St. Paul's discourse upon the hardening and healing of his people, like phraseology occurs. "Blindness in part is happened to Israel, *until* the fullness of the Gentiles be come in." Thus, again and again, this word "until" is heard, like a cadence, in the solemn strain of the Divine threatening, in which

Jehovah's voice seems to drop, for a moment, from the stern tones of anger and imprecation, to those of His "old love" and tenderness.[83]

But let it not be supposed that we have in the New Testament only inspired hints and implications concerning Israel's restoration. The eleventh chapter of Romans is a compact and well-reasoned argument upon this theme, conducting us step by step from sorrowful premise to triumphant conclusion. "*Hath God cast away His people?*" is the question considered. "*God hath not cast away His people whom He foreknew*," is the conclusion reached. And this upon two grounds,—present fact and future fulfillment. Though the *nation* has been cut off, there is "*a remnant, according to the election of grace,*" who have believed on Christ to their salvation, and therefore have been preserved in the favor and fellowship of God; while, on the other hand, those remaining outside this remnant have been hardened: "*the rest were blinded.*" But concerning this rejected majority, there is hope, because of the sure covenant of God. And though, like the branches of an olive tree, they have been broken off, we are told, first, that "*God is able to graff them in again;*" and, a little after, "*How much more shall these which be natural branches be graffed into their own olive tree.*" Not only possibility, but certainty, of Israel's restoration is thus predicated. And the argument culminates in the grand conclusion, "*And so all Israel shall be saved*"—an elect and individual redemption at last succeeded by a national and complete redemption. And this full recovery, it will be observed, is in connection with the second coming

---

[83] "O then that I
Might live, and see the olive bear
Her proper branches, which now lie
    Scattered each where,
And without root and sap decay,
Cast by the husbandman away,
And sure it is not far!

"For surely He
Who loved the world so as to give
His only Sonne to make us free,
Whose Spirit, too, doth mourn and grieve
To see man lost, will, for old love,
From your dark hearts this veil remove."
                    Henry Vaughan, 1654.

of Christ in glory. As it is written: "*There shall come out of Zion the Deliverer, and shall turn away ungodliness from Jacob.*"[84]

A typical man is often set before us in Scripture for our clearer instruction in regard to great events. And such was Paul in relation to the final redemption of Israel. He says of himself, the "blasphemer and persecutor" of Christ: "Howbeit for this cause I obtained mercy, that in Me first Christ Jesus might show forth all long-suffering, *for a pattern of those who should hereafter believe on Him* unto eternal life,"—ὑποτύπωσιν τῶν μελλόντων πιστεύειν—not *an ensample to,* but *a sample of,* those who should afterwards believe unto salvation. By the manner of his conversion he was constituted a kind of first-fruits, or prototype, of the Jewish harvest. Whether or not in this passage he refers explicitly to his kinsmen according to the flesh, we find, at least, that the circumstances of his own new birth were so unique as to constitute a special type. For, enumerating those by whom the Lord was seen after His resurrection, he says: "And last of all, as unto one born out of due time, *He appeared to me also.*" By the visible, glorious manifestation of Christ to his eyes, was this Hebrew of the Hebrews smitten with conviction; by the indictment of the Redeemer's personal wounds—"I am Jesus of Nazareth, whom thou persecutes"—was he brought to repentance and confession. When he "could not see for the glory of that light," then was the veil taken away from his heart, so that he turned to the Lord in the profoundest penitence.

"Behold, He cometh with clouds, and every-eye shall see Him, *and they also that pierced Him,* and all the tribes of the earth shall mourn over Him" (Rev. i. 7, R. V.). If, with most expositors we must understand "the tribes" in this instance to mean the kindreds and peoples of the world, we cannot so interpret the Old Testament prophecy of which this is a quotation. In the profound mourning, so graphically pictured by Zechariah, in which "every family apart" is seen sobbing out an uncontrollable grief, the scene is, by general consent, in the Holy Land, and the subjects the house of Israel. And what has come to pass? The bounds of another prophetic "until" have been attained for Jerusalem. "Upon the land of my people" God threatened thorns

---

[84] "The passage cannot be understood merely to denote the first appearance of Messiah as Isaiah xi.; but, in any case, the eschatological appearance of Jehovah is also conjoined in the Messiah."—Lange.

and briers, forsaken palaces, and deserted towers, "*until the Spirit be poured out upon us from on high*" (Is. xxxii. 15). That time has now been reached, and the word which God spoke by the mouth of Zechariah is fulfilled: "And I will pour upon the house of David, and upon the inhabitants of Jerusalem, the Spirit of grace and of supplications: and *they shall look upon Me, whom they have pierced, and mourn for Him*, as one mourneth for his only son, and shall be in bitterness for Him, as one is in bitterness for his firstborn" (Zech. xii. 10). The point of departure at last becomes the point of return. The wounds of Jesus were the death sentence upon national Israel; and now they become the source of life to that long-rejected people. For immediately upon the prediction of their mourning for Him whom they pierced, it is added: "In that day there shall be a fountain opened to the house of David, and to the inhabitants of Jerusalem, for sin and for uncleanness."

Nationally or individually, there is but one way of salvation for Israel,—the way of the Cross; and one way of repentance,—a total reversal of attitude towards the Nazarene. The Jews cried out: "*His blood be upon us and upon our children*;" and for this whole age that blood has been crying out for vengeance against them. By their own repentance and faith must that precious offering be turned from the blood of imprecation to the blood of cleansing. "*Not this man, but Barabbas*," they said, when the awful alternative was offered them; and Barabbas, the murderer and robber, has swayed them with his dagger, and pillaged them of their wealth, even unto this day. "*Not Barabbas, but this man*" must be their penitent confession before this spoiling shall cease. "*We have no king but Cæsar*," was their answer when the appeal was made to them, "Will you crucify your King?" And Cæsar after Cæsar has crucified, enslaved, and outraged them till, as no other, they have become a nation of sorrows and acquainted with grief. This fatal choice must also be reversed, and instead of it the acclamation be raised: "Hosanna to the Son of David! blessed is He that cometh in the name of the Lord!" Indeed, recalling Christ's prediction,—"Ye shall not see Me henceforth, till ye shall say, Blessed is He that cometh in the name of the Lord" (Matt, xxiii. 39),—we must remember that He gives us the key-note of Israel's repentance in these words. They are part of the Jewish "*Hallel*," sung at the Passover. The strain which immediately precedes this benediction is: "*The stone which the builders refused is become the Headstone of the corner. This is the day which the Lord hath made: we will rejoice and be glad in it*" (Ps. cxviii. 22-25). How glorious this song of Israel's consummated restoration! And what a heightening of the dramatic effect of that lurid picture of the overthrow of mystical Babylon, that, amid the rejoicing of the Church over the downfall of her great enemy, this "Hallel" is heard four times breaking in, as though Israel, too, were joining to celebrate the fall of the last and bloodiest form of Cæsar's kingdom, that from which both Christian and Jew have received their bitterest persecution! (Rev. xix. i, 3, 4, 6.)

As to the exact order of events connected with Israel's conversion and restoration, we must not speak too confidently. Some passages seem to make the Jews' repentance the occasion of the Lord's return, and others would appear to make the Lord's return the occasion of their repentance. Of the first kind is Peter's declaration to the crucifiers of Jesus: "Repent ye, therefore, and turn again, that your sins may be blotted out, that so there may come seasons of refreshing from the presence of the Lord; *and that He may send the Christ who hath been appointed for yon, even Jesus, whom the heaven must receive until the times of the restoration of all things*" (Acts iii. 19-21, R. V.). Here the Saviour's coming back is made contingent on the conversion of the Israelites; while, in the prophecy of Zechariah, that appearing in glory seems to be the producing cause of the Jews' repentance. From all that we gather, we judge that both conclusions are true,—that Israel will regather in their land in unbelief, as they are now beginning to do; that they will be brought into great tribulation through the assaults of enemies coming against them in siege; that in their utmost extremity they will cry out for their Messiah; and "then shall the Lord go forth and fight against those nations." His coming, however, will bring sorrow, as well as succor. "*His feet shall stand in that day upon the Mount of Olives, which is over against Jerusalem on the east.*" But those feet that bring deliverance will bring overwhelming conviction, as it is seen that they are the same that they once nailed to the cross. As He lifts up His hands for their help, "*one shall say unto Him, What are these wounds in Thy hands? Then He shall answer, Those with which I was wounded in the house of my friends*" (Zech. xiii. 6; xiv. 4). Thus while He comes to bring salvation to a repenting people, His coming will add repentance to repentance, as it brings home their terrible crime against their Messiah, so that "all the tribes of the land shall wail because of Him." But what joy shall give place to that lamentation, after their sin is purged! Now shall long-prostrate Jerusalem hear the summons: "Arise, shine; for thy light is come, and the glory of the Lord is risen upon thee."

The twin fact of Israel's restoration to God's favor is this of their restoration to their own land. To cite passages in proof of such restoration would be to quote whole chapters and entire books from the prophets, of whose writings this is the constant glowing burden.

This great consummation seems destined to occur in two principal stages, elective and national. First, a few are represented as being brought upon ships from their scattered habitations (Is. xviii.; lx. 9): "I will take you one of a city, and two of a family; and I will bring you to Zion" (Jer. iii. 14). These would appear to be a kind of first-fruits of the final restoration. And as sober judges of events see this gathering-out and gathering-home already taking place, it should be to us a sign and an earnest of the speedy realization of Israel's complete hope. After this partial restoration, we are led to expect the final and full regathering, a national movement, like the Exodus from Egypt, only far surpassing that in glory and power (Jer. xxiii. 3-5; xxxi. 8, 9).

This great restoration constitutes the true hope of the Israelite, as the return of the Lord does of the Christian. And it is very interesting to read, in the light of this fact, the closing chapters of the Old and of the New Testaments. In the one the promise is, "*Behold, I will send you Elijah;*" in the other, "*Behold, I come quickly.*" To the prepared people of His Church He *comes,* that He may receive them into the place which He has gone to prepare; to His long-disobedient people, Israel, He *sends* the prophet, that He may "turn the heart of the fathers to the children, and the heart of the children to their fathers." Accordingly, as for the Christian the communion is commemorative and anticipative, so is the Passover for the Jew. The Lord's Supper, by its solemn formula, is ever repeating, "Till He come;" and the Passover, with its vacant seat for Elijah, is ever saying, "Till Israel return." As the sprinkled blood and bitter herbs remind children and children's children of the Hebrew household how the Lord brought their fathers out of Egypt, they also recall evermore Jehovah's promises: "Therefore behold the days come, saith the Lord, that it shall no more be said, The Lord liveth that brought up the children of Israel out of the land of Egypt; but, The Lord liveth that brought up the children of Israel from the land of the north, and from all the lands whither He had driven them; and I will bring them again into their land that I gave unto their fathers" (Jer. xvi. 14, 15). Nothing that has yet occurred can be said to have fulfilled this prediction of "bringing them again into their own land." If the contrary be affirmed, how can we explain the finality and perpetuity of this restoration as affirmed in several parallel texts? "And I will plant them upon their land, and *they shall no more be pulled up out of their land which I have given them, saith the Lord thy God*" (Amos ix. 15; Jer. xxxi. 8-9; Ezek. xxxiv.-xxxvii.). And if any ask, "How can this be, considering the wide apostasy and practical surrender of these promises by such vast numbers of Israelites?" we must answer: How can it fail to be, since Jehovah, who made this promise, cannot lie? As though anticipating this incredulity of men, He has said, concerning the time when He makes a new covenant with His people, "to forgive their iniquity and remember their sin no more": "Thus saith the Lord, which giveth the sun for a light by day, and the ordinances of the moon and of the stars for a light by night, which divideth the sea when the waves thereof roar; The Lord of Hosts is His name: If those ordinances depart from before Me, saith the Lord, then the seed of Israel also shall cease from being a nation before Me forever. Thus saith the Lord: If heaven above can be measured, and the foundations of the earth searched out beneath, I will also cast off all the seed of Israel for all that they have done, saith the Lord" (Jer. xxxi. 31-37).

So great will be the glory of Israel's recovery, that the sorrow of His long rejection will seem as nought in comparison. Now will God comfort His people, saying: "For a small moment have I forsaken thee, but with great mercies will I gather thee" (Is. liv. 7). Instead of the sentence: "I have given the dearly beloved of My soul into the hands of her enemies," to His people, resisting no longer, He will say: "For as the girdle cleaveth to the loins of a man, so have I caused to cleave unto Me the whole house of Israel, and the whole house of Judah, saith the Lord, that they might be unto Me for a people, and for a name, and for a praise, and for a glory" (Jer. xiii. 11).

Not only shall their sun no more go down, but because the Lord is their sun, "the light of the moon shall be as the light of the sun, and the light of the sun shall be sevenfold, as the light of seven days, in the day that the Lord bindeth up the breach of His people, and healeth the stroke of their wound" (Is. xxx. 26).

IX.
THE MILLENNIAL KINGDOM.

IN the transfiguration—which is distinctly called "the Son of man coming in His kingdom"—we have a miniature presentation of the millennium. Moses and Elias, who appear with Christ in glory, prefigure respectively the risen and the changed saints translated and brought into one company at the appearing and kingdom of our Lord; while the disciples who stand without the cloud and behold His glory are typical of those in the flesh, the Jews and the nations, who will still be left on the earth after the rapture of the saints. What relation to this globe will the transfigured Church hold in the millennium? Some have maintained that she will be forever removed from this sphere, the world and its inhabitants being burned up together as soon as the Church is taken away. Others have held that while the ungodly will be utterly consumed at the appearing of the Lord, the earth, purified and renewed, will become the eternal and exclusive abode of the saints. Either view is extreme, as judged by a full collation of Scripture. It is plainly declared in Revelation that the saints shall "*reign over the earth*;" but that they will be absolutely bound to it, as now, by terrestrial gravitation, does not follow. "They that are accounted worthy to obtain that age and the resurrection from the dead . . . are angel-like,—ἰσάγγελοι,—and are sons of God, being sons of-the resurrection" (Luke xx. 36). Surely here is a suggestive hint for us. Angels visit this earth and mingle with its inhabitants; they have tangible forms, and accept material food, and exercise gracious ministries for those in the flesh, and yet they reside in a higher sphere. So may it be with the sons of the first resurrection,—in perpetual contact with the earth, but not inhabitants of it. Instinctively we turn for light on this subject to our Lord's forty days between His rising and His ascending. Though now in the resurrection body, He associated as familiarly as ever with His disciples: at one time holding high discourse with them concerning the things of the kingdom; at another eating in their presence of the broiled fish and honeycomb; to-day directing that cast of the net into the Sea of Galilee by which the multitude of fishes was enclosed, and to-morrow announcing the great commission in the mountain of Galilee by which the draw-net of world-wide missions was committed to His Church; and all the while maintaining that strangely double life in which He was now handled and inspected to prove his body to be literal flesh and bones, and now mysteriously withdrawn like a vanishing spectre. Here is revelation in a mystery concerning the glorified saints and their relation to the millennial earth. For the life of Christ is the life of His Church in epitome.

Reasoning from these hints, we gather that the millennial Church may hold a relation to the earth as close as that which we now maintain, and a relation to heaven as intimate as that which the angels enjoy. Perhaps there is more than poetry in the prophet's delineation of the Messianic glory (Is. xl. 31): "They that wait upon the Lord shall renew their strength; they shall mount up with wings as eagles; they shall run and not be weary; they shall walk and not faint:" celestial flight alternating with terrestrial travel, and each alike unwearying.[85]

What a realistic element in the promised victory of the saints it is, that they shall enjoy their triumphs in the very sphere where they suffered their defeats! This is according to the divine purpose. The millennium is called "*the times of the restitution of all things*" (Acts iii. 21). The steps in this restitution move slowly and steadily; but, because it is a *restoration*, each step forward is really a step backward towards the purity and perfection of the primitive paradise. All that was involved in the fall will be involved in the recovery: the soul restored to God by regeneration; the body restored to the soul by resurrection; and the earth restored to man by regenesis. Thus the rainbow arch of redemption bends back and touches the earth from which it springs,—"the sufferings of Christ, and the glory which should follow," both have their scene in the same material world. And remembering that the exalted Head and the mystical body have an identical destiny, we see how much is suggested by this fact. Christ returns in glory to the point of His earthly departure: "His feet shall stand in that day upon the Mount of Olives, which is before Jerusalem on the east" (Zech. xiv. 4). In His transfigured body He may now survey the literal scenes of His humiliation: Gethsemane, where He sweat great drops of blood; and Golgotha, where "by wicked hands He was crucified and slain;"

---

[85] "Captain Credence lifted up his eyes and saw, and behold, Immanuel came with colors flying, trumpets sounding, and *the feet of His men scare touching the ground.*"—Bunyans's *Holy War*, 17.

and the garden where He lay for two days buried. Heroic poetry, in its most presumptuous flights, has never dreamed of such a vindication for defeated warriors as this,—triumphing in a deathless body on the very field where the dead body was mutilated and entombed. And our Redeemer comes not alone in His victorious entry upon the earth: "Behold, the Lord cometh with ten thousands of His saints to execute judgment upon all, and to convince all that are ungodly among them of all their ungodly deeds which they have ungodly committed, and of all their hard speeches which ungodly sinners have spoken against Him" (Jude 15). Christ's confessors, who, being reviled, reviled not again, but committed themselves to Him that judgeth righteously, may tread again the very judgment halls where they listened in silence to the hard speeches of ungodly sinners who condemned them to death; may stand on the very spot where the earth once drank up their witnessing blood, or tread under foot the very soil with which their martyr-ashes once mingled.

Will the glorified Church hold relation to mortal men still living on the earth? They who deny this, and suppose that the whole human race will be swept from the globe and destroyed at the coming of Christ, quote words of terrific import for such a view (2 Thess. i. 7). But if we balance Scripture with Scripture, the conclusion is otherwise. For not only is it taught that the advent judgments fall especially on apostate Christendom (Matt. xiii. 40, 41), but with equal clearness that Christ's coming issues in the conversion of Israel (Zech. xii. 10; Rom. xi. 26), and through Israel in the conversion of the Gentiles (Rom. xi. 12-15; Is. lx.). We conclude, therefore, from a wide collation of Scripture, that after the translation of the Church, two classes will still remain living on the earth,—the Jews and the nations. And as the glorified saints have now become "kings and priests unto God," they must exercise rule and ministry over some besides themselves, and over whom but these? Here Scripture is clear and harmonious with itself. Immanuel now takes "the throne of His father David," that He may "reign over the house of Jacob forever." But He is not alone in His kingly rule over Israel. Of His risen saints it is written that "they lived and reigned with Christ a thousand years." His glorified Bride sits by Him in His throne, Queen-consort with her enthroned Lord; nearer to Him than any other as "the wife of the Lamb." Now is fulfilled that Scripture which cannot be broken: "Verily I say unto you that ye which have followed Me in the regeneration,"—the regenesis,—παλιγγενεσία, "when the Son of man shall sit in the throne of His glory—*ye also shall sit upon twelve thrones judging the twelve tribes of Israel*" (Matt. xix. 28). In this dominion of the risen saints there doubtless is order and precedence according to the degree of suffering and loss endured for Christ. The apostle band would seem to have especial preëminence; next the martyr company, whose long waiting for the avenging of their blood is at last rewarded; and saints and believers of all generations, who have been counted worthy to obtain that age and the resurrection from the dead. Israel is still in the flesh, though converted, purified by long trial, and brought at last into loyal subjection to Messiah. Through her as a redeemed nation, and through her exalted city as capital of the world, the Son of David will now extend His blessed sway to the ends of the earth. "For out of Zion shall go forth the law, and the word of the Lord from Jerusalem. And He shall judge among the nations, and shall rebuke many people; and they shall beat their swords into ploughshares and their spears into pruning-hooks; nation shall not lift sword against nation, neither shall they learn war any more" (Is. ii. 4). At length, through this benignant consummation, the righteous government for which the suffering nations have sighed will have been reached. The last attempt at human rule, like all before it, will have miserably failed, and men, despairing of self-help, will finally be prepared to accept the benignant rule of God, that perfect theocracy in which Christ the Lord shall be King over all the earth. We have said in a previous chapter that election is not the end of grace, but the means to a vastly higher end. This ultimate purpose here comes into view. The elect Church, glorified with her Lord, and the elect nation Israel restored and converted, now take up the work of universal redemption. Have we pondered the deep suggestiveness of the apostle's saying: "He hath raised us up together, and enthroned us together with Him, *in order that He might show forth to the ages which are coming the exceeding riches of His grace in His goodness towards its in Christ Jesus*" (Eph. ii. 7).[86] The garnered wealth of redemption, the holiness, and faith, and love gathered up from generations of chastened experience, and now displayed in the transfigured Church,—what may be the impression of this upon the generations of the age to come? At last the Son of

---

[86] "That God in the future order of things, that is, in the kingdom of God,—in which the glory of the faithful, which is hidden here below, will be made visible to all,—may manifest the overwhelming richness of His grace."—Olshausen's *Paraphrase*.

God is fully manifested in "the manifestation of the sons of God." He has come "*to be glorified in His saints and to be admired in all them that believed*" (2 Thess. i. 10),—the raised and enthroned Church being as a mirror in which His majesty is reflected and displayed. Now will be seen "*what is the riches of the glory of His inheritance in the saints*" (Eph. i. 18). And we may believe that, as the Queen of Sheba was astonished at the splendor of Solomon, and attested her admiration by rich gifts, so the generations yet unsubdued to Christ at the opening of the millennium, may be filled with wonder at the exhibitions of redeeming grace now visible in the perfected Church, and at the riches of His forbearance as manifested in converted Israel, so that they shall be moved to take up, concerning Immanuel, the beatitude of this admiring queen: "Happy are thy men, happy are these thy servants which stand continually before thee and that hear thy wisdom. Blessed be the Lord thy God which delighteth in thee to set thee on the throne of Israel: because the Lord loved Israel forever, therefore made He thee king to do judgment and justice" (1 Kings x. 8, 9). These triumphs may not be gained at once; but they will be effected with a rapidity of which we as yet know nothing, so that literally a nation shall be born in a day. For two new conditions will now be brought in,—conditions utterly unknown since the fall of man: the binding of Satan and the universal outpouring of the Holy Ghost. Let us try to conceive of the astonishing changes which will thus ensue in the complete repression of "the spirit that now worketh in the children of disobedience," and in the unrestrained operation of the Spirit of truth and holiness now poured out upon all flesh. What will have now come to pass is not simply an exchange of malign influences in the earth for more benign, but the actual dethronement of "the god of this age,"[87] and the unhindered reign of Christ in his stead. Thus there is a complete reversal of conditions: "the Prince of Peace" holding absolute sway in the dominion where the "Prince of the power of the air" has so long triumphed. Now will be ushered in the real golden age of which the weary nations have so long dreamed,—the true Sabbath-keeping for which the people of God have waited. If our readers have been inclined to

---

[87] "That which ceases by the binding of Satan is the cohesive power of evil, by which it has been able to become an historical and motive principle in the development and in the life of nations, by which it has proved itself a ruling power on earth. Instead of that now comes in the development of the power of the glorified Church of God."—Karsten.

put a mark of interrogation against any of our millennial anticipations, we have only to remind them that when the chief apostle bounds forward in thought to this period, and speaks of its "far more exceeding and eternal weight of glory" (2 Cor. iv. 17), his language becomes well-nigh untranslatable, he so joins hyperbole to hyperbole—καθ' ὑπερβολὴν εἰς ὑπερβολήν—in his effort to express its transcendent blessedness. "The uniquely beautiful, the eternally true, the highest good, must be fittingly made manifest upon an earth whereon they have been so long ignored; and as that earth has so long crowned with thorns its lawful King, it must contemplate Him yet once again in His full beauty. It is this blissful period to which prophecies like Isaiah xi. 6-9, xxxv., lx., lxv., and others appear to us to point. It will be the time in which the kingdom of God rules upon earth. Purified by suffering and conflict, the Church of God now shares in the triumph of its Head: the Bride finds her rest, after her long wanderings in the desert, on the bosom of the Bridegroom. It now becomes apparent that the kingdom of God is in reality a *power* in every domain with which it comes in contact, and that the highest manifestation of the truth calls forth a life such as without this is nowhere found on earth. In a word, it is the time of the Christocracy ever more triumphantly unfolding itself; the realization of the Ideal, of which the old Theocracy in Israel was only the shadow; a realization, however, which in nothing detracts from the universalistic character of the Saving Revelation now brought to completion."[88]

The relation of the three classes of men in the millennium has been compared to the threefold division of the tabernacle. The Bride of Christ, the glorified Church, is the Holy of Holies, exalted into equal fellowship with her Head.[89] Converted Israel is in the relation of the Holy Place, and the nations which come up to worship Jehovah stand as in the court of the Gentiles. Only we must be reminded how completely the veil of the Holiest is now rent asunder, so that as the millennial triumph advances all peoples are embraced

---

[88] Van Osterzee, *Christian Dogmatics*, p. 799.

[89] "How beautifully does the prophet Isaiah (Is. iv. 5) suggest the Bridal relationship of Christ to His Church in the millennium! The shekinah glory has returned: 'A cloud and smoke by day, and the shining of a flaming fire by night.' And now it is said, not as in our common version: 'For upon all the glory shall be a defense,' but 'Upon all the glory *shall be the marriage canopy*.'"

in the light of God's favor. The cloud of glory—symbol of Jehovah's presence—was first contained within a narrow ark in the wilderness; then, as the Temple of Solomon was dedicated, it filled the whole house, so that "the priests could not stand to minister by reason of the cloud" (2 Chron. v. 14); in its final outreach it will embrace the world in its effulgence, and the whole earth will become a Holy of Holies. Then will the kingdom of God be fully consummated; the blessed predictions of righteousness and peace contained in the seventy-second Psalm will be no longer chanted only in the music of the Levites, but they will be set to the measures of literal accomplishment, and sung out in the strains of triumphant experience: "All men shall be blessed in Him; all nations shall call Him blessed." At length, in a restored creation, will Messiah see of the travail of His soul and be satisfied. Thus will the Psalm of redemption be finished: "And let the whole earth be filled with His glory. Amen, and amen. The prayers of David the son of Jesse are ended" (Ps. lxxii. 20).

But we have outrun our argument, and must return to what has been passed over.

Beside Jew and Gentile and Church of God, there is still another sharer in the millennial redemption; a dumb partner who is yet to find utterance when "the hills shall break forth into singing, and all the trees of the field shall clap their hands." "Often" says Goethe, "have I had the sensation as if Nature, in wailing sadness, entreated something of me, so that not to understand what she longed for cut me to the heart." We understand what her longing is, and what is to be God's final answer to it. "For we know that the whole creation groaneth and travail eth in pain together until now, . . . waiting for the adoption, to wit, the redemption of the body" (Rom. viii. 23). Earth bears the wound received through man's transgression, and the brute creation travails in anguish with fallen humanity. Deep as is the mystery of punishment for sin, the punishment of no sin, as witnessed in animal suffering, is even more inexplicable. "In Adam all die:" not only all persons but all things. But as man and creation fell together, so must they rise together in the time of redemption. Earth will then lay off her soiled week-day garb and put on her Sabbath dress, and, with her singing robes about her, take up again that anthem which was heard when the morning stars sang together, and all the sons of God shouted for joy. "Cursed is the ground for thy sake, thorns and briers shall it bring forth to thee" (Gen. iii. 17, 18), is the sentence which for six thousand years has remained as a sign and testimony to God's judgment upon sin. But then: "Instead of the thorn shall come up the fir tree, and instead of the brier shall come up the myrtle tree: and it shall be to the Lord for a name, for an everlasting sign that shall not be cut off" (Is. lv. 13). The beauty of holiness and the eternal harmony of redemption must be displayed where the dishonor of sin has been most visible. Therefore this globe, which has so long served as a grave for man fallen, will now serve as a temple for man upraised; yea, more, as Anselm says: "The whole earth, which carried in its lap the body of the Lord, will be a paradise."

With such predestined glory before her, what wonder that Nature should be found taking her place with Christ and the Church as an eager expectant of the Advent? If we could bring out the full original of that passage, "*For the earnest expectation of the creature waiteth for the manifestation of the sons of God*" (Rom. viii. 19), we should behold a delineation so graphic that, as Godet has said, "A sculptor of any imagination and genius might carve a statue of Hope from it." The picture is this: "*Nature, an unwilling slave to vanity and corruption, stands, impatient of her bonds, with uplifted head, scanning with longing eye the distant point of the horizon from which she looks for help, her hands stretched out to grasp and welcome the redemption into freedom and perfection which she yearns for and confidently expects.*"[90]

It is necessary to emphasize this truth of the rehabilitation of the earth on philosophical as well as on spiritual grounds. For we know not how to vindicate the ways of God to sober thinkers, if this material world is to end in catastrophe instead of regeneration. A vague shadowy heaven beyond the stars, to which man as a bodiless immortal spirit is to be finally transported, has little meaning or attraction for the ordinary mind. And we are free to say that such a conception is a triumph of Gnostic philosophy over scriptural revelation,—the philosophy which finds man's highest happiness in release from this material body, and therefore, logically, the race's highest attainment in deliverance from this material world. While this notion is widely prevalent in the Christian Church of our day, we deny that there is anything inspiring

---

[90] Dr. Samuel Cox on Rom. viii. 19.

or victorious in it.[91] Instead of the apostolic prayer for the perfection of our "whole spirit, soul and body at the coming of our Lord Jesus Christ," it places our hope in the dismemberment of this human trinity: it proposes a truce with the grave, willingly surrendering the body to its possession, provided only the soul may be eliminated in the dissolving chemistry of death, and float away to some realm of happy shades. Instead of rejoicing in the beatitude, "Blessed are the meek: for they shall inherit the earth," it makes haste to yield all right and title to this globe, if only the saints may be released from its gross environments, and soar to worlds unknown. Even so lofty a thinker as Edwards gives full sway to this idea in his "History of Redemption," where, speaking of the end, he says: "Thus Christ's Church shall forever leave this accursed world to go into the highest heaven, the paradise of God. . . . When they are gone this world shall be set on fire and turned into a great furnace, wherein all the enemies of Christ and His Church shall be tormented forever." Is this an alluring conception of redemption, that in its final issue it will have turned what was made to be a Paradise for man's delight, into a purgatory for his torment? We should call this the apotheosis of divine failure, rather than the crown of divine redemption. Yet it is the logical outcome of that philosophy which considers the spiritual to be everything, and the material nothing. We hold that it is infinitely honoring: to the Creator to believe that in the end He will be found tabernacling in a restored world, from which He has wiped away the last vestige of sin, and in which He has silenced the last discord of rebellion.[92] If the problem of human destiny is to be worked out to

---

[91] It is a one-sided spiritualism which can conceive of no perfectly consummated blessedness save in a heaven distant as far as possible from this earth. Infinitely more acceptable, and more worthy of God, is the Biblical conception that this earth, too, which, through sin laden with the curse has been made the scene of grace, has, as well as other worlds, a peculiar destination to accomplish in the realization of God's adorable plan; and that the gulf shall entirely cease to be, which at present exists between heaven and earth."—Van Oosterzee, *Image of Christ*, p. 491.

[92] "Upon two distinct grounds we may believe that the earth will ultimately be made new,—First, that having been brought under the bondage of corruption, not of its own will, but by the sin of man, it is embraced in the scope of redemption; it is to enter into 'the liberty of the glory of the children of God' (Rom. viii. 21). Second, that God having made man, body and soul, and appointed the body to be an essential element in humanity, He will so order the material world that it shall minister in the highest degree to all his needs. If the body be raised into a higher condition through resurrection, there must be a corresponding change in its

a successful issue only on some yonder side of creation, and in such unknown terms and quantities that even the spiritual Christian cannot comprehend it, how impossible it will be to justify God's dealings to men! In treating of the doctrine of future life, it may be questioned whether modern theology has not so far withdrawn from a sober and Scriptural materialism as to be carried into an attenuated, and for the most part incomprehensible, spiritualism. We believe, on the contrary, that in setting forth the judgments and rewards of the future, God has expressed them in conditions which even the men of this world may understand if they will.

That there must be a baptism of judgment-fire for the earth, preparatory to this anointing with millennial joy, is plainly revealed. How difficult it is to explain the predictions of Scripture on this subject, we need not say. "The day of the Lord" of which Peter writes—"in the which the heavens shall pass away with a great noise, and the elements shall melt with fervent heat, the earth also and the works that are therein shall be burned up"—is evidently a long period, embracing the entire age, from the second advent to the close of the millennium. It is *within* this era that these burning judgments occur. But the fire is for purging, and not for annihilating, since the announcement immediately follows: "Nevertheless, we, according to His promise, look for new heavens and a new earth, wherein dwelleth righteousness" (2 Pet. iii. 13). In the prophecy of Isaiah we have a glimpse of this renewed order: "For, behold, I create new heavens and a new earth, and the former shall not be remembered nor come into mind" (Is. lxv. 17). Now Jerusalem is seen restored and made a perpetual joy in the earth; a warring creation has been tamed, and the wolf and the lamb are found peacefully feeding together. But though life is wondrously ameliorated and prolonged, so that one a century of age is counted an infant,—"The child shall die an hundred years old,"—immortality has not yet been reached for the whole race on earth. The goal of death has been pushed far onward, but not abolished; and though for the risen Church death has been swallowed up in victory, it still has dominion over men in this globe during the millennium.

---

material environments,—the new creation serving as a means to higher knowledge of God, and to the continual enlargement of man's conception of His power, wisdom, and goodness."—Rev. S. J. Andrews, *God's Revelations to Men*, p. 361.

But looking on to the end of this millennial period we behold the final and perfected order in which mortality, with all its sorrowful accompaniments, has at last been swept away: "And I saw a new heaven and a new earth; for the first heaven and the first earth were passed away: and there was no more sea" (Rev. xxi. 1). Now the climax of blessedness has been reached for the world and all that dwell therein. As the opening of the millennium witnessed the bridal of the Church with Christ, its close will witness the bridal of the earth with heaven. Then the redeemed were caught up into the clouds to celebrate their nuptials with their Lord; now the Lord comes down to our globe to celebrate the nuptials of the earth and sky: "And I heard a great voice out of heaven saying, Behold, the tabernacle of God is with men, and He shall dwell with them, and they shall be His people, and God Himself shall be with them and be their God. And God shall wipe away all tears from their eyes; *and there shall be no more death, neither sorrow, nor crying, neither shall there be any more pain; for the former things are passed away*" (Rev. xxi. 3, 4).

From all we have thus considered, our inference is, that the redemption of the earth will begin with the return of the Lord from heaven at the opening of the millennium; but will only be perfected at the end of that period, when death shall be forever abolished, and there shall be no more curse. The millennial kingdom is thus redemptive, not only for the race, but for the earth,—the final chapter in the great restoration which is to usher in the eternal state. Though far surpassing all which we now know in blessedness, the millennium will not be a faultless condition. Sin and sin's agencies will still have a certain sway; for Satan will yet once more incite rebellion before being finally and forever cast into the lake of fire (Rev. xx. 3-10). But after that the eternally perfect, the faultlessly holy, condition will be reached. Of this condition we can as yet only catch transporting glimpses, and speak in stammering accents. It is the time when God shall be all in all, and the whole world brought into unwavering obedience to His will. The long-suffering Church forever married to her Lord; Israel, once hated and forsaken, now made an "eternal excellency, a joy of many generations;" the Gentiles, who long lay at the gate full of sores, carried by angels into Abraham's bosom; and the world, with all its reconciled inhabitants, lying forever on the breast of God.

"Earth, thou grain of sand on the shore of the Universe of God; thou Bethlehem, amongst the princely cities of the heavens,—thou art, and remainest, the Loved One amongst ten thousand suns and worlds, the Chosen of God! Thee will He again visit, and then thou wilt prepare a throne for Him, as thou gavest Him a manger cradle; in His radiant glory wilt thou rejoice, as thou didst once drink His blood and His tears and mourn His death! On thee has the Lord a great work to complete!"

www.ingramcontent.com/pod-product-compliance
Lightning Source LLC
Chambersburg PA
CBHW020423010526
44118CB00010B/390